The
SEASONED
GARDENER

Liz Zorab

Permanent Publications

Published by
Permanent Publications
Hyden House Ltd
13 Clovelly Road
Portsmouth
PO4 8DL
United Kingdom
Tel: 01730 776 585
          International: +44 (0)1730 776 585
Email: enquiries@permaculture.co.uk
Web: www.permanentpublications.co.uk

Distributed in North America by
Chelsea Green Publishing Company, PO Box 428, White River Junction, VT 05001, USA
www.chelseagreen.com

Designed by Two Plus George Limited, info@twoplusgeorge.co.uk

Cover photo by Jason Ingram, www.jasoningram.co.uk

Printed in the UK by Bell & Bain, Thornliebank, Glasgow

All paper from FSC certified mixed sources

The Forest Stewardship Council (FSC) is a non-profit international organisation
established to promote the responsible management of the world's forests.
Products carrying the FSC label are independently certified to assure
consumers that they come from forests that are managed to meet the social,
economic and ecological needs of present and future generations.

British Library Cataloguing-in-Publication Data
A catalogue record for this book is available from the British Library

ISBN 978 1 85623 264 7

PRAISE FOR THE BOOK

Some garden writers give their readers a peek over the garden fence to share their gardening knowledge, skills and experience. Liz Zorab's intimate and detailed writing makes you feel that you're actually kneeling down on the damp soil right next to her as she gardens or sat in her kitchen as she prepares, stores or cooks the bountiful produce grown in her own garden. Her extremely detailed understanding of growing leaps out of each and every inspirational sentence. I was constantly torn between wanting to go out and grow more produce or to set about cooking in my own kitchen. Liz Zorab is a tour de force in garden writing.

Mike Palmer
Chair of Garden Media Guild,
host of Mic the Gardener podcast

A radical voice in contemporary growing, in *The Seasoned Gardener* Liz Zorab gently leads the reader through an entertaining year of advice, delivering an impressive case study proving that growing in tune with nature is better for us and for wildlife.

Jack Wallington
landscape designer, nature writer

Not only does Liz's book have a friendly 'over-the-fence' commentary like you're chatting with a gardening friend, it's also really informative and packed with nuggets of information that will help you get the most from your plot. Did you know elephant garlic takes longer to sprout than regular types, or that growing carrots between them will keep carrot fly away; Liz did, and she'll share all that knowledge page after page.

Rob Smith
gardening columnist, presenter,
product development and Horti Expert

Feel inspired and empowered as Liz Zorab guides you on a journey through the growing year in this refreshingly different gardening book. Liz's extensive knowledge and deep connection with nature and the gentle rhythms of the seasons shine through the pages, which are packed with detailed advice, beautiful photography and her characteristic grounded optimism and excellent good humour. A joy to read, it's a book to return to again and again.

Stephanie Hafferty
no dig homesteader, award winning garden writer,
organic gardener, food writer and educator

With sage advice, thoughtful introspection, and a peppering of her characteristic humour, Liz guides you along a gentle and personal journey through the gardening year. You'll be transported through the seasons and learn much from her years of experience and how she embraces lessons learned. Her message of slowing down and savouring small moments makes this book as much about growing vegetables as it is about connection to the natural world.

Tanya Anderson
Lovely Greens, author and YouTube gardener

This is an awesome resource for gardeners of all levels. Liz uses her personal experiences in the garden to provide practical advice and valuable insights throughout the different seasons. I was impressed by Liz's resourceful and creative approach to gardening, which works with nature and aims to create a productive, diverse and enjoyable space. The different ways Liz uses her produce has definitely given me some ideas to make the most out of the things I grow. The storytelling in the book is engaging and captures Liz's humor and relatability, providing inspiration and encouragement for anyone interested in growing an abundant garden.

Kalem – The Kiwi Grower
YouTube gardener

Liz Zorab shares so evocatively how beautiful, joyful and productive a permaculture garden and farm can be. The photos ooze gorgeous edible diversity and every page is a trove of invaluable growing tips. Walking with Liz through the seasons of her gardening is an inspirational invitation to a kind of freedom and calmness that comes when you trust and garden with nature, eat what is fresh, listen to your own rhythm and begin with an observant pause and deep respect for all life.

Morag Gamble
founder of Permaculture Education Institute,
writer, film-maker and permaculture educator

As an avid gardener, I was thrilled to discover *The Seasoned Gardener* by Liz Zorab. This comprehensive guide covers everything from beginner gardening tips to advanced techniques, all written in an easy-to-understand and enjoyable style. Not to mention the book is organized by season, making it easy to find exactly the information you'll need at any time of year. Whether you're a seasoned pro or just starting out, *The Seasoned Gardener* is a must-have addition to your gardening library.

Jason Smith
Cog Hill Farm

At times, gardening can feel overwhelming. However, *The Seasoned Gardener* helps to break things down, season by season, month by month in a calm and concise manner. From seed starting, to attracting wildlife to your garden, it feels like Liz is in the room with you, sharing her knowledge and giving you the tools to confidently tackle your own garden.

Jason Williams
Cloud Gardener UK

I love this book. It's packed full of warmth, gentle humour and oodles of very accessible and practical gardening advice to encourage and inform the reader. A recommended read.

Kim Stoddart
award winning journalist, editor of *The Organic Way* magazine
and author of *The Climate Change Garden*

In a little over one year, Byther Farm has developed from an excitingly bare patch of Welsh mountainside into a truly productive, beautiful space. This book takes you there. Redefining how we look at the gardening year, Liz brings her perfect mix of knowledge and joy for what can be achieved on the land. It is a personal account of the seasons that is packed with practical information, inspiration and wit, borne out of many years of growing. Just as you can see Liz reflected in Byther Farm, you can feel her warmth and guiding hand with you in this book.

Niall McCauley
Niall Gardens YouTube channel

Following Liz through the seasons, we see the garden take shape while gaining the knowledge to shape our own. Just like in *Grounded*, Liz's passion for growing jumps off the page, making *The Seasoned Gardener* a joy to read, and an easy book to recommend.

Serina Nell
You Can't Eat the Grass

This book on growing organic food is like having a humorous and very knowledgeable friend with you as you read. It does not make you feel that you are not doing enough, but gives practical help for you to get the best from each season that is within your scope. The section on weather and water is especially relevant today. Nothing beats practical wisdom from an author who believes in her gardening and has experimented to know what works and what will work for your own unique situation. Easy to read, inspirational but practical and for both beginners and existing gardeners.

Liz Wright
Editor of *The Country Smallholder* and smallholder herself

CONTENTS

For Mark, Cecily, Hunter and Magnus

FOREWORD
BY HUW RICHARDS

I remember when I got the phone call announcing with palpable delight that the new homestead was now theirs! Liz and Mr J had been through quite the moving ordeal, but at long last their new home was secured. The next thing I heard was "when can you see it?", and so a week later, with a car load of carefully potted plants taxied from the original Byther Farm in Monmouthshire, I opened the gate and drove into the new chapter of Byther Farm; Carmarthenshire edition.

What first struck me was the blank canvas Liz had to work with – both a blessing and a curse. We all know the paralysing feeling of staring at a blank page and wondering how to start filling it with words – heck, that is how I started this foreword – and the same paralysis can happen when you get a blank piece of land begging for love and diversity. But the blessing of a blank canvas is realised when you are fuelled with passion and creativity, which Liz definitely is.

After a whistle stop tour of, "This will be the vegetable garden, food forest can go here, flower garden there, new hedge area by that fence, perhaps bees in this field, oh this is the duck house...", I could almost feel the land thanking her for breathing new life into it. Fast forward some two years, the ground is rapidly regenerating into a paradise for people and nature. Liz has the experience of creating four other gardens over the years and is almost single-handedly transforming Byther Farm into a hidden gem. What was a bleak mountainside is now a masterpiece in motion, and *The Seasoned Gardener* is a physical copy of the experience Liz is using to achieve this, allowing you to also create your own masterpiece, no matter the scale you're working on.

Having written a foreword to *Grounded*, I was honoured to be asked to also write one for *The Seasoned Gardener*. Being a nosy soul, any excuse to read an advanced copy of a fellow gardening author's book is interesting, and so I accepted the foreword request. What I didn't yet realise was just how much I would get from reading this book.

What I love about this book is that this is clearly Liz's voice through and through; *The Seasoned Gardener* captures her quirks, humour, musings, and all! Secondly, Liz has gone where few vegetable gardening books have gone before; starting the growing season towards the end of autumn. Whilst we often associate spring as the start of the new season, the preparation for success begins from October right through winter, taking advantage of time for less plant-tending and more garden-prepping.

Every month is broken down into a mini handbook approach to the garden, and the quantity of valuable information packed into this book is no mean feat. Practical tips and advice are peppered throughout, intertwined with thoughts and inspiration to tie everything together.

Having experienced both of Liz's recent gardens in fine detail, I can confirm she isn't a one hit wonder, she is the real deal. I am so excited that you are about to read a book, whatever your growing experience, that is a treasure trove of information for anyone passionate about gardening.

HUW RICHARDS

Gardening video creator (YouTuber) and best-selling author of *Veg in One Bed*, *Grow Food for Free* and *The Vegetable Grower's Handbook*.

INTRODUCTION

Looking around our garden in Monmouthshire, almost without exception people said that it must be a lot of work or that it must be a full-time job to attend to, and with a little smile, I either nodded gently in a non-committal way or deflected the comment. The reality is that I aim to create gardens that don't take much looking after and are far from a full-time job. I spend much less time actually working in the garden than you might imagine. I do enjoy great swathes of time pottering around outside, but for much of it I am fully occupied by sitting quietly, watching and listening to the wildlife around me.

I would very much like to change the narrative around activities in the garden, with less use of words like work and jobs and more emphasis on the language of art, enjoyment, fulfilment and experience. Using words that properly express our relationship with our gardens and the wider environment would change the way we perceive the

activity-filled time we spend surrounded by and immersed in nature. Rather than having feelings of obligation, it could become something we look forward to and actively seek to do.

Mr J (my husband) and I live in an oceanic temperate climate, approximately equivalent to US Hardiness Zone 8a. Geographically the UK is as far north as Canada, but our weather is milder because the air is warmed by the Gulf Stream as it travels across the Atlantic. The southernmost parts of the UK enjoy milder weather than the north and the western areas receive more rain than the east. Never being too far away from the sea, the air is almost constantly humid and we rarely have incredibly hot summers. We live in the south-west of Wales, so we have mild, wet weather. On the whole our climate is never excessively hot or excessively cold. Depending on where you are in the UK, it can become quite dry or stay rather damp, but in general we are fortunate to have a good growing climate. Cool loving plants thrive for most of the year and those that love warmth can be coaxed into growth with the use of a greenhouse, polytunnel or windowsill, and planted outside during the summer months.

As a child and teenager, I saw ornamental gardens that were filled with annual bedding plants planted in neat rows and patterns forming a living, almost three-dimensional picture, but they didn't resonate with me. When I discovered the work of Gertrude Jekyll, Christopher Lloyd and Rosemary Verey (among many others), I felt an instant warmth towards their gardens. They were stuffed full of flowers, leafy plants and grasses that all jostled for our attention and yet at the same time complemented each other, letting the plants next to them shine in their moment of splendour before our attention was drawn away to others bursting into colour. This style of carefully planned planting that gives the appearance of 'plant it wherever there is a gap' has stayed with me over the last 40 years and I still strive to create a garden that looks effortlessly grown. More recently I have been inspired by the prairie style plantings of Piet Oudolf and plan to incorporate some of those ideas into our new plot of land.

Likewise, the vegetable gardens of my youthful experience were planted in regimented rows and ruled over by chemical applications. Farms were in the process of, or had already completed, the stripping out of hedgerows and ploughing up of great swathes of land to plant monocultures, changing the landscape around us for decades to come. Hedgerows and scrubland provide essential habitat for wild birds, mammals and insects. The impact of their removal, together

with other practices of industrial farming, has become evident as numbers of birds, pollinators and other wildlife have declined exponentially. Reinstating hedges and living edges around our gardens provides a sanctuary for those birds and animals and helps to redress the balance in a very small but positive way.

Byther Farm in Monmouthshire was the fourth garden that I've created from scratch; with each attempt I get a little closer to my ideal garden. In our small space on this beautiful planet, we aim to provide a safe haven, with a medley of plants and environments in which life, in all its forms can thrive. Our new home in Carmarthenshire brings with it new challenges and new opportunities to learn, to grow and to thrive. My long-term aim is to create a productive landscape that is also filled with ornamental plants and flowers. A place where productivity and pleasure mingle side by side, each supporting and enhancing the other. I've learnt so much as I've developed each new garden and I hope that some of my ideas prove useful to you.

Woven into my approach to gardening and, more generally, my approach to life are the guiding ethics and principles of permaculture. Sometimes it is obvious and 'in your face', at other times it's more subtle, gentle and quiet, but nonetheless, I have found the premise of caring for the earth, caring for people and caring for the future, a sensible, doable and kind way to live. These guiding ethics are not exclusive to permaculture; they were not just invented in the late twentieth century; they appear time and again in teachings and beliefs across the world and throughout time. I see the twelve permaculture principles as guidance and a roadmap that is inspired by and works with nature, to help us design and create a cohesive, functional environment that minimises our negative impact on the land in which we live. If we, as individuals, can reach the point where we have no negative impact or better still, leave a positive one in our wake, the planet will stand a better chance of surviving our ever-growing population's demands upon the finite resources available.

Following on from *Grounded*, the purpose of this book is to share the rhythm and patterns of my gardening year. Unlike many gardening books which work from January to December and guide your sowing and planting times, this book starts in autumn, when gathering food for consumption during the rest of the year is at its peak. Most of the fruit and vegetables that I mention in this book are grouped according to when I enjoy them the most – at the point of harvest. The personal journey in *Grounded* focussed on physical healing; in this book, I share my observational and emotional journey throughout the gardening year.

BEAUTY AND THE FEAST

Long before I discovered the joys of eating our own fresh, seasonal, nutrient-packed vegetables, I tended an ornamental garden. When I first started gardening, I went to bed each night and read a handful of gardening books over and over again. I studied an RHS vegetable gardening book with far more attention and interest than any book I'd been presented with at school or college. Although I didn't imagine I'd end up growing so much of the family's food, I was fascinated by the gardening techniques explained. Snatched moments of quiet between duties of caring for my toddler, were spent thumbing through Dr. D G Hessyon's range of *Expert* books, to which I will still refer on occasion. Their dog-eared condition lays testament to the sheer volume of use they've had in the hands of a grower eager to learn. From the comfort and security of my armchair, I became a keen gardener with a good

understanding of basic techniques, theories and principles of horticulture. Meanwhile, the garden outside my door was little more than a weedy patch of grass and an even more weedy border with a few flowers in it. But I was smitten. I very quickly discovered that I am one of those gardeners who looks beyond the flaws, weeds and chaos and only sees the beauty of the flowers or the way the grasses sway in the wind.

The next joy in my gardening learning was to discover the writing of Christopher Lloyd. An intelligent, eloquent author with a sense of playfulness, he still makes me chuckle aloud. His many years of experience, of honing his skills, seemed to give him a confidence in the knowledge of what he did and didn't like in a garden. One passage from his book *The Well-Chosen Garden* has stuck in my mind for 40 years. He wrote about dwarf conifers, which had been incredibly fashionable in the gardens of the time and for the decade beforehand. His thoughts on the subject made the penny drop in my mind,

that we don't have to go with the flow of gardening vogue. It may seem obvious now, but as a new gardener and a young woman, I hadn't understood that I could express my personal tastes and my personality through the garden.

I have never been gifted as an artist, nor have I been very skilled in creative arts, despite being keen to have a go. I can't draw very well and even painting by numbers is a bit beyond my ability. I used to sew competently, as long as you wanted to wear curtains or patchwork cushions (which I don't recommend as a good look for shopping on the high street!) and for a long time I created tapestry cushions from canvas and wools. Nowadays my eyes struggle to see the holes in a canvas or to even thread a needle, but the love of putting colours together, to contrast or blend, to highlight or enhance, continues in the garden. I'm also not too bad at putting flowers and foliage together in a vase. It seems that my flower arranging skills are good enough to have been asked to create flower baskets for the funerals of friends' parents.

I provided the floral arrangement for my mother-in-law's coffin. It wasn't necessary, we could have paid a florist to do it, but it allowed me to express my love for her and 'do something' at a time when I had little else that I could offer to be helpful. Somewhere during my discovery of gardening, I realised that I was rather good at putting plants together in growing beds to make them look aesthetically pleasing, at least to my mind.

BEYOND BOOKS

It wasn't long before I started to visit other gardens, for inspiration and to gain a deeper understanding of what I'd been reading. The way that I look at gardens when I visit them is to wander around, seemingly aimless, taking in the general feel of the garden and the vague layout. Then I'll head to specific areas that I've spotted on my first walk through and spend time observing, soaking up the atmosphere created by that particular planting arrangement, in that setting, at that time of year. There are usually some 'oohs' and 'ahs' at the showstoppers and the accent plants that shout to be seen before anything else. But those aren't the ones that intrigue me the most. I am more interested in the supporting cast, the quietly understated plants that form a backdrop and setting, because without them, the stars of the show wouldn't shine nearly as brightly. If a garden is created solely from the showy plants, they lose their impact and, rather than standing out from the crowd, they are the crowd.

I admire gardeners who can put together a collection of plants that allow different blooms or foliage to have their moment of stardom and then take on a supporting role for the next plant to have its moment. Even more, I admire gardens where this is done without the need to dig everything up and change the display twice a year, or more.

I visited Barnsley House near Cirencester repeatedly. Now a hotel, it was at the time home to Rosemary Verey. I saw how clipped hedges and plants could be used to create patterns and geometric designs or used to contain borders, providing a neat edge to what otherwise might be perceived as a jumble of plants. I saw how vertical accents, climbing plants and permanent structures could add not just height, but a sense of depth in a garden. The only part of her garden that I didn't aspire to was the lawn. I don't much like them; they require a huge amount of work and resources to maintain and I find them neither beautiful or useful.

I visited a garden in Lancashire; I wish I could recall its name. I do, however, still remember the borders of flowers alternating with rows of topiary box cones. Again, it was the combination of formal lines contrasting with billowing flower borders that struck a chord in my heart.

When I rented a house from the local council in Gloucestershire, the generous garden was a corner plot and it was surrounded by a hedge so typical of council estates. The *Lonicera nitida* hedge was years old and ridiculously thick and had grown far higher than I wanted it to be. What I discovered is that it takes time and effort to clip those hedges into crisp neat shapes and that I wasn't very good at it! It grew tall enough to block out much of the light to the plants hidden behind it and never really looked as good as I would have wanted. That experience taught me that if I was going to have hedges around the edge of the property, it probably needed to be a mixed species hedge that didn't rely too much on my care and attention for it to look good. And also, that I might need to redefine what I meant by 'a good-looking hedge'.

Nowadays I prefer a row of hedging with a mixture of plants and an understorey of wildflowers, that hasn't been tidied too much and provides flowers, berries or nuts. Part of me still wants to see those neat, controlled straight lines, but the more sensible side knows that I just don't have the capacity or interest in maintaining a monoculture of plants that offer shelter but little else to the wildlife with which we share our home. In the few places where a single species hedge is planted, I supplement it by underplanting with a wide selection of species to offer more variety to the wildlife.

At the end of the last century, I moved to Wales, to a Victorian villa with a long garden. I divided it into four with a central path and another path crossing it half way down the garden. The pathways were made using reclaimed red bricks. I didn't have to go very far to get them.

About two weeks after we moved into the house, there was a violent storm with very strong winds. After a disturbed night's sleep, I woke in the morning to find that the wind had blown over the Victorian wall that divided our garden from the lane next to it. A stretch about 1.2 metres (four feet) high and 20 metres (70 feet) long had collapsed into the lane and urgently needed moving. With the help of a local builder, I picked up the bricks and dumped them into the garden to clear the lane. These lovely old bricks, mostly misshapen and flawed,

Niall McCauley (Niall Gardens) tends a one-acre ornamental garden in Ireland that was created by the previous owners. He has cared for this space for a couple of years and is slowly revitalising and rejuvenating it, adding his own features and style as he does. It includes an area that he calls the 'secret garden'. It has clipped hedges containing a mixed border and I admire how neat it looks when he's recently trimmed the box hedge. Although many of the plants in the border are now either very mature or over-mature for the intended purpose of this area of his garden, it won't take him too long to restock the beds and bring them back to their former glory or find a new twist to enhance it.

Image courtesy of Niall McCauley

were not any good for building a house, but had been adequate for the garden wall. Now they would become the path. I laid them in a basketweave pattern directly onto the soil, which I had firmed by walking up and down the slight slope of the garden where I wanted the path to be. The base for the path wasn't level and consequently neither was the path, but I loved it all the same.

The two large areas nearest to the house were flower borders and the lower part of the garden was for fruit and vegetables. I bought a couple of large box plants in a sale at a garden centre and took a great number of cuttings to grow into new plants. The idea was to line the edges of the path and create that neat boundary that I'd seen and loved in others' gardens. Box is a relatively slow-growing plant, but my little hedge managed to fill out and grow to knee height before too long. I filled the flower borders with my favourite plants and with anything and everything that I was offered by generous local gardeners. The result was a riot of chaotic colours and textures. But it never felt completely cohesive and tended to look like I'd just dumped a load of plants into the ground to see how they worked together. For the most part, it looked like this because that is exactly what I had done.

Visits to Powis Castle in Mid Wales were always a pleasure; the scale of the place, the incredible restoration and maintenance of the garden left me in awe of the gardening team. The garden has towering yew hedges, open vistas and intimate corners, colourful herbaceous borders and a white garden. Although I haven't visited Powis Castle for over 15 years, I can still recall some of the planting combinations and how much pleasure they offered.

I have come to understand much more about what it is that I liked in those gardens that I visited. Above all, I liked the results that could be achieved by a team of gardeners who tended the gardens very regularly. Trying to reproduce another's garden is likely to fail on many levels. My great failing was to expect that I could reproduce that style and complexity of planting with just one person gardening sporadically.

SEASONAL WORK AND CASUAL LABOUR

Over the last 30 years I have begrudgingly accepted and then, more recently, positively embraced my body and brain's need to slow down and rest during different periods of the year. Just like a plant that becomes dormant in the winter, conserving its energy for a flush of new growth when the warmth and light returns in spring, my body wants to do the same. I've often wondered how plants that provide the

earliest blooms, like snowdrops and crocuses, find the strength to start growing in the cold and dark depths of winter. I'm grateful that they do because their appearance reminds me that it won't be too long before the spring arrives once again.

I used to struggle my way through the darker days of late autumn and winter, becoming increasingly depressed and angry with myself for my inability to put in a full day's work. Even in early spring I would be frustrated that I just couldn't achieve as much as I 'should' in a given day. What a 'full day's work' should look like used to be determined by an employer, but after I took the leap to being self-employed, the prescribed number of work hours was a self-inflicted goal. I know that, even at the best of times, I am still hopelessly inaccurate with my estimate of how long a given task might take to achieve. Equally, I am all too often completely ignorant of the processes it would take to complete a task, so my estimate of 'it'll only take…' is, without fail, far fewer hours than a particular job actually needs. And even though I know I need to factor in time for breaks, cups of tea, meals (including time to cook them), the number of available daylight hours and stopping for inclement weather, in my mind a task is almost done in the time I take thinking about doing it!

The disparity between what I wanted to do and how much I felt physically and mentally capable of doing was enormous and that led to me feeling inadequate and dissatisfied.

Over time I noticed the pattern in my behaviour, this slowing down in the autumn and winter, and in vain, searched for reasons outside myself. Eventually, quietly and reluctantly, I realised that my energy levels were less under my conscious control and were in reality, affected by the seasons. I have Seasonal Affective Disorder that impacts me both mentally and physically. Acknowledging this was liberating.

I still haven't got the rhythm of the year quite right, I still try to achieve too much at a time when my body guides me to rest, but that, I think, is a result of post-industrial societal conditioning. In a time when technology gives us instant access to so many things – shopping, news and information are available 24 hours a day – it is easy to forget that just because it is there, doesn't mean we have to use it, nor are we obliged to make ourselves available all of the time. Like the fragile petals of a poppy that fall within a day, or the heady scent of sweet rocket that is almost imperceptible during the day but fills the warm evening air, we can shine in the appropriate moments and conserve our energy at other times.

Another major change that I have made in the last year or two, is to learn to ask for and to accept help in the garden. Somewhere along the line I had got it into my head that it was 'my garden, my responsibility' and that the workload should be mine alone. What tosh! Yet another self-imposed limitation. When we were

Monty is my constant companion in the garden

preparing to put our Monmouthshire home on the market, I wanted to make sure that I had removed the woven plastic weed suppressing membrane from the food forest. I had promised myself that I would do this a couple of years after first laying it down, and after five years, it was well embedded, riddled with pernicious weed roots and covered in a deep layer of wood chips, all adding up to making it incredibly heavy and cumbersome to remove. I just couldn't lift it. I responded to an advert on social media from a team of young people who had recently started a garden clearance business. They were duly called upon for help and were on site once a fortnight for four months. They lifted the membrane, cleared brambles, cut back weeds and working alongside them, we got an enormous amount of work done in a relatively short time. Lesson learnt.

It wasn't long after moving that I found 'Dave the Hero', who now works with me once a week to keep on top of the general maintenance tasks on the land of our new home in Carmarthenshire. With our time freed from some of the strimming, weed whacking, hedge trimming, grass cutting and clearance tasks, Mr J and I can concentrate more on the practicalities of setting up our new gardens and renovating our home. Later on, the additional help will allow me to be more productive in the garden and to concentrate on running the business of our smallholding.

In the past, we have had help from friends, who have spent a day here and there, planting, moving wood chips, cutting hedges and a host

of other tasks that have been much more fun to do with a friend or two than to tackle on my own.

My dear friend Jane and I have been gardening side by side for 35 years or more. We don't see each other as often as I'd like, but we talk at length on the phone at least once a month and over the last few years, Jane has come to stay with us for a weekend annually. In 2021, when we were once again allowed to visit friends with caution, Jane took the long train journey to our new home and we spent a day in the garden filling a 70 foot long row in the food forest with trees, shrubs and herbaceous perennials. I invited her to return to help plant a vast number of daffodil bulbs, but the weather, family commitments and her paid employment meant that it was 2022 before she could return to visit us again. I may not have chosen my invitation wording very well because

nobody jumped at the chance to spend a day or two on a cold, wet and windy mountainside, crouched over in the mud to put 1000 or more daffodil bulbs in the ground!

My vision for the daffodils was to plant them on each side of a track, between our fields, that we have nicknamed 'The Runway'. Inspired by the cheerful greeting of nodding daffodil heads on the track leading to my sister's home, I too wanted the sight of the post and rail fences lined with yellow and cream flowers joyfully announcing the arrival of spring.

In late autumn of 2021, it took around ten hours for Dave and I to plant the daffodil bulbs. It was worth the effort and I'm looking forward to watching the display increase year after year as the bulbs naturalise along The Runway.

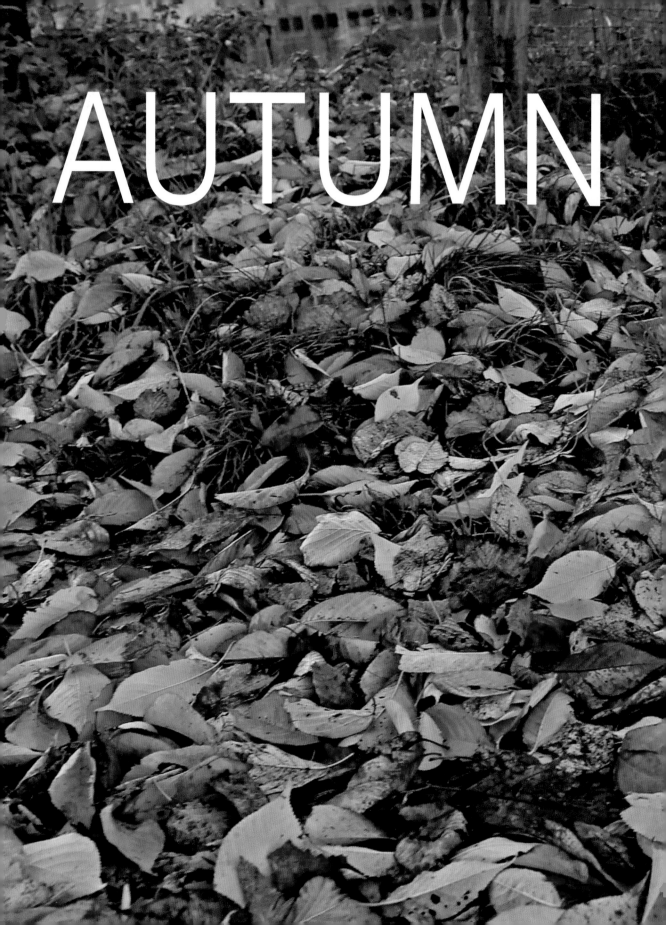

At the end of summer, there is a time I think of as 'The Pause'. It's that short period, when for a handful of weeks, the heavy warmth of fragrance-filled air hangs over the garden like an invisible blanket of joy. The light is rich and soft in colour and shafts of early evening sun highlight a myriad of insects, all busy in their activities, like cosmic dust all around us. The warmed earth reflects the heat back at us and being barefoot in the garden is a pleasure. Without a doubt, this is my favourite time of year.

SEPTEMBER

For me, like many others, the gardening year starts somewhere towards the end of autumn. September, however, often feels like an extension of the summer, the only difference being that my days are increasingly spent in the kitchen rather than in the garden. The focus has shifted to harvesting, preparing and preserving food for the months ahead. The abundance of food is moved, bit by bit, from the heavily laden garden to the house. Our kitchen becomes enveloped with the sounds and aromas of preserving as empty jars are filled and the cupboard shelves replenished for another year. Demijohns are lined up, first on the kitchen work surfaces and then, because we have limited space in the house, they progress to a corner of the bathroom floor. I started putting them in the bathroom in our previous home, mainly because the bathroom had under-floor heating which I thought would help speed the fermentation process. And now that we live in a smaller house, keeping them tucked in a corner next to the airing cupboard seems to make sense.

Our meals are filled with fresh produce, salads, stir-fry dishes and the lighter tastes of late summer. Soft fruits like raspberries and blackberries are picked daily and the first of the apples are picked from the trees and collected from the ground. Each year, the first blackberry and apple crumble has a significant meaning: a tangy and sweet combination that reminds me of the warming meals we'll enjoy in the months ahead.

In the garden, as areas in the growing beds are cleared of their harvest, a mulch of enriching compost is applied. Or at least that is the theory. I never have enough homemade compost to cover the bare soil, so instead I heap on used duck bedding or wood chips. Most of the vegetable beds are grown as polycultures, so harvesting one crop doesn't leave a large, easy-to-access clear space. Over the autumn season mulches are applied in a patchwork pattern across the beds as they are gradually emptied of their annual growth.

As the humidity increases, the conditions improve for the spread of mould and fungal diseases and so often our tomatoes and potatoes succumb to late blight. Squashes fatten on their vines as if in a mad dash to the finishing line. And although the process of ripening can take a couple of months, it is obvious that the huge scrambling, sprawling vines, often turning white with powdery mildew, are winding down, having achieved their purpose of developing seeds and continuing their genetic line.

RUNNER BEANS

There are usually more runner beans than we know what to do with. I wish I was more disciplined. I wish I could believe myself when I think that twelve plants are enough for our family of two. A row of a dozen runner bean plants provides us with fresh beans for slicing and eating just minutes after harvesting them and also with plenty of beans for storing, either dried or frozen, for use in the cooler months. And yet, almost without fail, each year I grow twenty or more plants of a variety called White Lady. Apart from a couple of years when I first started gardening, I have always grown this variety; it has a delightful taste, creamy flowers and produces a white bean inside the green pod. I far prefer them to red or orange flowered varieties that produce a dark red bean.

In addition to the White Lady runner beans, I also grow twenty or more Greek Gigantes bean plants. They are not grown for the green pod, but for the huge white bean that forms in the pods. They have a buttery potato flavour and since first trying them six years ago, they have rapidly become one of our favoured alternatives to potatoes in the colder months when we've eaten all the potatoes we have in storage.

The problem with growing two runner bean varieties is that, to be blunt, runner beans are rather promiscuous! So good are they at ensuring the continuation of the species, that the pollen from the flowers of one variety can mingle with another and cross pollination will occur unless the beans are growing a very good distance apart. In the past, my beans have cross pollinated with those growing in a neighbour's garden, which isn't a problem because we still have beans to eat, but it is a problem if you want to save seeds for planting the next year.

Over the last five years, the size of the beans inside the pods of the plants on each of the rows of beans has changed. Some of the 'White Lady' beans produce very large seeds and some of the Greek Gigantes beans could easily be renamed Mediocres.

In our new garden, I have started with fresh, purchased seeds so that once again we can have the delicious, buttery Greek Gigantes beans we have come to love in stews and casseroles and in the occasional bean burger. I have also brought with us several pots of older bean plants that I dug up from our last house. These old bean plants were from my original sowing of bought-in seeds. Each year I have cut the stems about 10-15cm (4-6 inches) above soil level and mulched heavily to provide some protection from the winter frosts. Although not every plant survives the cold, wet winters, enough survive to regrow the next year, providing stronger, bushier plants that give an increased harvest.

Runner beans easily cross pollinate. If you grow more than one variety and save the seeds, the resulting plant may be a mixture of your varieties.

French beans do not usually cross pollinate, so you can grow several varieties in close proximity, save the seeds and they are likely to remain true to variety.

And because they are regrowing from the root ball each year, they are not cross pollinated and are our original sowing reappearing time and again. Of the ten plants that I brought with me to Carmarthenshire, just two have survived after being neglected in pots for the last twelve months or so. However, I am delighted that these two stoic survivors have been planted into the ground to continue their lives in the new garden.

Even though I know that the beans will cross pollinate, I still intend to grow both varieties because I value each one for their different qualities.

I've tried several different support systems for beans, two favourites are made using a V of either canes or strings. This allows the beans to hang down away from the supports making them easily accessible for picking. In Monmouthshire, I created a pergola style support from recycled wood and used baler twine tied between the top side bars and a second set of bars fixed a little way above soil level. It reminded me of a harp and that is how we referred to it.

CHANGE OF COLOUR

The pale and pastel colours of the summer blooms in the garden give way to the warmer, richer colours of autumn flowers. The frothiness of tiny white and pink flowers on delicate stems are replaced by bigger, bolder blooms, like those of dahlias and clusters of flowers that look like a mound of blossom such as *Hylotelephium spectabile* (formerly known as *Sedum spectabile*). Cosmos, which have flowered

for the previous two months or so, seem to revel in the slightly cooler weather and produce masses more cheerful, daisy-like flowers. The sounds of bees, wasps and other insects visiting the flowers makes the garden a joyfully noisy place. It is as though nature gives us a prelude to the symphony of colours and textures to come during the autumn months.

COMPOST HEAPS

Compost is made through bacterial action, luckily, we need to do very little to it and nature does all the work. Billions of microscopic bacteria will feed on the materials that you add to the compost heap; worms and slugs will eat the materials and excrete them to add to the rich mixture. Every compost heap is teeming with, mostly unseen, life that over a period of time turns leaves, stems and woody materials into dark brown earth-like compost for you to add to your soil. Compost is perfect for using as a mulch, to feed the soil and to improve both water-retention and drainage.

The most basic way to make compost is to spread out the leaves, stems, vegetable and fruit peelings on the soil and leave them to break down, but this isn't ideal in our gardens. The debris can attract vermin, get in the way of the very space you want to plant in and, most importantly, it won't break down as efficiently as using a compost heap. When the materials are gathered in a heap, pile or container, decomposition can occur more quickly.

Compost heaps also need sufficient water and oxygen. A basic cover over the heap, like a plastic sheet, old carpet, even several layers of cardboard (replaced regularly) will reduce the chances of the heap becoming waterlogged, but equally, it should not completely dry out.

To encourage further decomposition of the materials and to improve the oxygen content, the heap can be turned. This process is simply mixing the contents of the heap and is most easily done by moving the heap from one place to another. This is why you often see not one, but two or more compost containers next to each other. The top layer and outer edges of the heap are turned to the bottom and centre of the heap to encourage decomposition of those materials too. If you don't have space to turn the heap from one spot to another, use a garden fork to stir and mix the compost heap.

To create the best compost, use carbon and nitrogen materials in the ratio of 30:1 by weight. Realistically, I can't imagine anyone weighing material going into the compost heap, and I make compost by adding some carbon materials (browns) and some nitrogen-rich materials (green) in layers.

When there are too many greens, there's a risk of anaerobic decomposition and you end up with a slimy, stinky compost heap. It can be improved by adding more carbon materials. With an excess of browns, the pile takes a long time to break down and is more likely to use fungal action, as with leaf mould. While there's nothing wrong with that, the healthiest of gardens will have composts made using both fungal and bacterial action, thus adding both types of soil life back into the garden soil.

Brown materials include cardboard, shredded paper, egg cartons, newspaper, dried leaves, straw, wood chips and sawdust.

Green materials include annual weeds, manure, coffee grounds, kitchen scraps and peelings, discarded plants from the garden, grass clippings and feathers.

There are two basic types of compost heaps, neither is right nor wrong, they are just different.

- ▸ **Cold composting**. Compost heaps are made by adding materials to them as you find them. It may take many months to fill a compost heap if you have a small garden and little access to other materials to compost. Even in our large garden I use cold composting heaps, because I find them more convenient. Cold composting is a slow process; it can take 18 months or more for all the materials to break down into rich, dark compost. The downside to cold composting is that it does not kill weed seeds in the heap, so you need to be more careful about selecting materials to add to the cold compost heap.

- ▸ **Hot composting**. Compost heaps are more often started with a volume of materials at once. The combination of nitrogen rich and carbon rich materials, together with water and oxygen will encourage bacteria to work on the heap quickly and a heat is obtained in the centre of the heap, which will rise and then fall. Added to the speeding up of compost making, the heat will kill most seeds in the heap, thus ensuring that you aren't spreading seeds of unwanted plants across your garden when you use the compost.

I also have a 'bad compost' heap and to this I add any materials that I don't want to risk being returned to the soil. Annual weeds in flower or those that have gone to seed, and grass clippings containing a large number of seed heads are placed into the bad compost heap. Rather than using the finished compost on the soil of the garden, I leave it in situ and use it like a raised bed and grow plants like squash in the top of the heap. It's worth noting that you can grow plants in any compost heap, squash in particular seem to like a nutrient-rich compost heap in which to grow.

SWEETCORN

My first taste of sweetcorn came from a tin. The label had a picture of a tall green man on it and that was the benchmark of what I expected sweetcorn to taste like. Because I have a sweet tooth, I rather liked it, but I wish I had known many years earlier, just how good freshly picked, quick-to-the-pan sweetcorn is. There's a bite to the skin of the kernel that gives way to the smooth, sweet centre and an aroma that you can almost taste.

At some point in September, most of the sweetcorn is ready to harvest and I then process it for storage. I grow a variety called Special Swiss, having tried several other varieties, and to date I, by far, prefer the taste of this. I usually harvest and process about ten cobs at a time, so that none of them are sitting around the kitchen quietly becoming starchy. I blanch the sweetcorn cobs in boiling water for about three minutes and then leave them in a colander to cool for about five minutes. Then they are plunged into cold water to stop the cooking process. Once they are cool enough to handle, I carefully cut the kernels away from the core and spread them out on a tray before putting them into the freezer. Once the sweetcorn is frozen, I transfer it into large bags for storing. This makes it easy to grab a handful of frozen sweetcorn for meals throughout the year. I have also pressure canned some sweetcorn, but I find the texture of the vegetable less appealing when it has been preserved this way.

Every year I marvel at the roots of sweetcorn plants. They seem so close to the surface of the soil, that I wonder how they can anchor such tall plants adequately. Their secret is a dual root system of fibrous roots that keeps the plants in place in all but the strongest of our summer and autumn winds. I used to lift the roots after harvesting, putting the stalk and roots into the compost heap to break down very slowly over the next two or more years. But to disturb the soil as little as possible, I now cut the stalks close to the base, leaving the roots in situ. They will decompose over the coming months, adding nutrients and organic matter to the soil and where the roots have pushed through the soil, there will now be channels that allow air to circulate or rain to drain into the lower soil levels. The thick and sturdy sweetcorn stalks decompose much faster if they are broken up, either chopped into small pieces or smashed with a hammer to break them apart before being put into the compost heap. Alternatively, they could be put through a chipper.

I think the best way to eat sweetcorn is to put a pan of water on to boil before you harvest the cobs, pick the cobs, hurry back to the kitchen, strip away the leaves that encase the cob and plunge it into the boiling water as quickly as possible.

The main reason for the haste is not my greediness or impatience, although those factors may play a part, but that the cob starts to deteriorate once taken from the stalk. The sugars in each little kernel begin to turn into starches, making the vegetable tougher and less sweet.

With a little careful planning, it is possible to have fresh
cabbage or brassica leaves available all year round. There are
annual cabbages that can be harvested throughout the year
and there are also some wonderful perennial alternatives.

CABBAGE

Cabbage has come a long way since my childhood. No, that's not entirely true. It's not that the brassicas have changed, but that my understanding of how to prepare and cook cabbage has improved. Those hard balls of pale green leaves tend to be limited to use in coleslaw, but savoy and red cabbage get treated with reverence in our house.

Of all the vegetables that we grow, I am most fond of growing brassicas. I'm not necessarily most fond of eating them, but that's not the point. I get so much pleasure from watching a small round seed transform into a young seedling. I enjoy the process of transplanting brassicas into their permanent positions, although I might not say that after I've lovingly firmed the soil around 50 or more brassica plants in a weekend. But most of all, I am thrilled at the work of art that cabbages are and at the joy of harvesting brassicas in the late winter and early spring.

Cabbages are incredibly useful. They store for a couple of months or more if kept in the right conditions and are versatile in the kitchen. Cabbages sown in March or April are usually ready to harvest from September onwards. I use red cabbages for two different dishes: as a basis for a fruit-laden coleslaw and also braised in red wine, with apples, sultanas and warming spices as a side dish for meals throughout the year. I often harvest several red cabbages at a time to allow for batch cooking, because if I've got the oven heated, I might as well fill it and make the most of the energy being used. On the other hand, I tend to harvest green and savoy cabbages one at a time as needed. I've tried slicing and freezing savoy cabbage and it's better than having nothing, but only just!

As yet, I haven't managed to be quite organised enough to have fresh cabbage all year round from annual plants, but I've come fairly close and that's a good feeling. There is usually something to harvest from the brassica family, even if it's not an actual cabbage. Brussels sprout tops, sprouting broccoli leaves or kale flowers all allow us to extend the harvesting season of a brassica plant. Growing perennial cabbage offers further opportunity for a long harvesting season.

To store cabbages, remove the large outer leaves and trim the stalk to within a 3cm (1 inch) of the cabbage head. Place into nets, tights or mesh bags that allow air to circulate around them. Hang in a cool shed, garage or store room. Hanging them ensures better air flow and lifts them away from potential predators and vermin. Check them regularly and remove any that have mould or any type of infestation.

To keep pears for eating later, store them in a fridge. I use the bottom drawer; I think they are referred to as salad drawers. Place the pears carefully, one at a time, into the storage space and keep cool. Try not to bruise them when harvesting or storing as that will make them vulnerable to rotting. Stored in a cold place like this, pears can last for a number of months. To ripen them to eat, they need to be taken out of the fridge and kept at room temperature for a week or two. Using this method, we have often had homegrown pears on Christmas Day.

AUTUMN FRUITS

Depending on the weather and growing conditions, some apples and other tree fruits are ready for harvesting. Our former neighbours had a couple of fabulous apple trees, I wish I knew which varieties they are. One in particular produced huge apples that had a pink blush to their flesh and were superb when made into apple sauce or diced for pie filling.

The pears on our duo pear tree would hint at being ready to harvest during late September. Pears rarely ripen on the tree, which helps when it comes to storing them for use at a later date. To tell if a pear is ready to be picked, cup it gently in the palm of your hand and raise it to the horizontal position. If it comes away from the tree, it is ready to take into the house to ripen. Leave it in a warm room for a week or two and it will become a juicy, tasty fruit.

In our new home, there were no pear trees or any other fruit trees for that matter, except for one gnarly old damson near to the house. I have since planted dozens of fruit trees, but it will take a year or two for them to start producing enough fruit to store. And in the meantime, we'll enjoy whatever fruit we can get from them.

SWAP AND CHANGE

I have a circle of friends who are happy to share the abundance and to exchange their harvest glut for something that they don't have. I am surprised at how regularly we all manage to grow one or two types of vegetables very well and between us are able to supply our families with an array of different herbs and vegetables. Knowing that we were moving home in 2021, I had harvested and stored in the freezer and by pressure canning, as much food as I could during 2020, but some foods were just not going to keep long enough. Our friend Tony planted and grew a year's worth of onions for us, which he brought to us just before we moved. Arriving here knowing that we were secure in so much of our food for a year was a blessing.

In our new home, we have already found friends with whom we can swap our surplus food. Not only that, but during our first few months at the new site, friends arrived with homegrown organic food for us to enjoy, like salads, spinach, chard and squashes. Once again, I am reminded that growing a network of like-minded friends in your area is every bit as important as growing some food in the garden.

If, after I've filled veg boxes (ordered via a local food co-operative) and swapped food with friends, there is still a large amount left over, I try to find ways to use it before making the decision to return the glut to the earth via the ducks or the compost heap. I could make pickled vegetables, but as neither Mr J nor I like eating pickled vegetables, there seems little point in using my time and energy to create something that won't be eaten. I do however make rich chutneys and relishes. We don't eat a great deal of them, so a few jars each year is sufficient for our needs.

Much of what I do in these autumn months is about taking stock, assessing and preparing for a better managed garden the next season.

> An abundance of food is one thing, a wasted glut is another. Whenever I find that we simply have too much of one type of vegetable, I make a note in my journal to look at the quantities that I am growing and to adjust the amount sown or grown in the following year.

SPLITTING HEADACHE

In my imagination, August is a really good time to collect and gather firewood for the winter. After a summer of being in the warm air, it is likely to be reasonably dry and easy to handle. Well, that's the theory! The reality is that August is not a great time to sort out wood for the winter: it is either too wet to want to gather wood, or it's too hot for the onerous task of splitting logs.

It is usually the end of September before I start to ask Mr J to get some logs sorted for the following year. We take wood to a covered space to allow it plenty of time to dry out. Wood gathered this year will be used in 15-24 months' time. Having a wood burner is a luxury for us, we do not need it to supply heating, but we both enjoy the look of a fire in the wood burner and the cosy atmosphere that it creates in our home. More recently, the cost of fuel has made us think twice before switching on the heating and it makes far more sense to use wood that is available to us for no cost except for our time and effort.

When we first moved into our home in Monmouthshire, the previous owners left us some wood, already split, dried and neatly stacked, but after the first winter we needed to cut and split some more. Luckily, our tree surgeon friend, Tim, came to the rescue and brought his log cutting saw. It was a huge affair that fitted onto the back of his tractor and made short work of chopping up the tree trunks and branches that we had lying under cover. All we (read Mr J) needed to do was to split the logs and I (we) could stack them to allow them to dry out properly. We had found a splitting tool, a conical wedge, that needed to be hammered into the end of each log so that the pressure of it entering the wood forced the log into two. We also had an axe to chop and split the pieces further.

Now call me a killjoy if you like, but my idea of fun is not spending several weekends in a row splitting wood, listening to the occasional expletive from Mr J and the much more frequent potty-mouth comment from me as I gathered up bits of wood that had flown all over the gravel yard. The novelty of preparing our own firewood had worn off quickly, very quickly indeed. But without the cash to buy ready split wood and with the gift of logs and branches from Tim on a regular basis, we were destined to continue in this grumpy pattern for years to come.

In autumn 2020, I decided that I couldn't bear another year of fighting with the wood when I needed to be harvesting and storing food for the months ahead, and I splashed out on a hydraulic log splitter. It felt like an extravagance, but on the other hand, it also felt like the sensible thing to do.

We assembled the log splitter, apart from a cage contraption that fits around it to prevent logs flying off at odd angles, and then got side-tracked by other pressing needs. Shortly afterwards, we made the decision to move home, so there seemed little point in splitting a load of wood just to leave it behind. We decided to buy nets of wood for the very short time it would take to sell our home and move. That was the first of many mistaken assumptions!

Selling our old home happened quickly, there was plenty of interest in it and we agreed a sale within a few days of marketing it. Finding a suitable new home was not a quick process, however, and the purchasing process seemed to drag on and on. The spring was cold and in desperation to not spend more money than needed on logs, I went out to the barn to attempt to use the log splitter. I carefully read through the instructions which said 'fill the oil chamber with lubricant oil before use'. And then helpfully added 'oil not included'. I headed back into the house, muttering rude words. The new log splitter had become the equivalent of a new and shiny ornament in the stable area. Mr J ordered the correct type of oil which was duly delivered, tucked away on a shelf and quietly forgotten about as we concentrated on packing up our belongings. By the time we had finally purchased our new home, we had bought netted logs for the whole of the winter and spring and we still hadn't worked out how to use the log splitter. Occasionally, we all make purchases that aren't quite right. Sometimes the machinery isn't up to the job you have in mind and sometimes, we aren't up to using the machinery. I feel in this case, it was the latter. But no matter, we would take it to Carmarthenshire and learn to use it there.

What to sow in September

☐ Fava bean | broad bean

☐ Spring cabbage

☐ Chinese cabbage

☐ Lettuce and other salad leaves

☐ Spring onion

☐ Overwintering onion (sets)

☐ Pea

☐ Potato (first earlies for a mid-winter harvest)

☐ Radish, summer and winter varieties

☐ Spinach

☐ Turnip

OCTOBER

Having taken careful note of which foods I've grown too much of and those which I'd like more of in future years, October is a good time to think about which seeds to order for the next growing year. Between continuing to process and store harvested food and mulching beds to protect them over the winter months, many a happy hour is spent deciding which of the seeds I already have enough of and which varieties I want more of. Poring over the pages of seed catalogues, albeit online rather than in print, is a joy and inevitably, I get drawn in by the photos of richly coloured vegetables, fruits and flowers.

I have an embarrassing number of packets of seeds. I am, without a doubt, a seed hoarder. It is not a good practice and not something to be proud of. As a precious resource, I think seeds should be valued and treasured, but also they should be used. If they aren't sown at some point, they are no more than decorative baubles.

REALITY BITES

In our new home, we have considerably more space in which to grow plants, but I don't have additional hours in the day to sow, prick out, transplant, water or tend to the plants, so the number of annuals that I can grow is limited to the time I have available. Potentially, one day we'll be in a position to find regular help in the vegetable garden, but for now, I need to be realistic about my capacity to work in the gardens.

In Monmouthshire, I started growing a small range of perennial vegetables to discover which ones we liked and which, for us, were interesting but unlikely to become firm favourites – a polite way of saying that we aren't going to eat them. There are a handful of perennial vegetables that we like and that could replace the annual equivalents: Taunton Deane kale, walking onions (*Allium × proliferum*), and a short-lived perennial Asturian tree cabbage all deserve a place in our new garden. I also want to further explore 'nine-star broccoli' and Babington's leek (*Allium ampeloprasum bulbiferum*). They will grow side by side with annual varieties, providing us with a range of tastes and forms of these veg for the kitchen. Some vegetables usually grown as annuals, like runner beans and garlic, I'll continue to grow as perennials, and other veg, like asparagus and rhubarb, I have only found in a perennial form.

In addition to the home kitchen garden, I've created a half-acre food forest. It's filled with perennial planting of fruit and nut trees, fruiting shrubs, herbaceous perennials – both edible and ornamental, – climbers and ground cover plants. In the first few years, I want to keep any weeds surrounding these plants under control. Plants establish better when they have little competition for water or for nutrients in the soil. Once established, they will mostly have to fend for themselves. I will walk through the food forest regularly to remove any pernicious weeds, but by and large, the growth of the established plants will create shadier spaces at soil level, which in turn is likely to reduce weed growth.

My good intentions are clear in my mind, but my experience in Monmouthshire on a much smaller site was very different. Weeds simply grow faster and stronger than my enthusiasm to remove them!

The reality is that I am not a neat and tidy gardener who can create and maintain a well-ordered plot, in which weeds are banished the moment they dare to show themselves. All those packets of seeds that I have stored in an orderly fashion are indicative of how a part of me would like the garden to be, but I want to achieve more

Be honest with yourself about the amount of time and energy you have to give to your garden and create a space that you can tend within your given time constraints.

than I have time or energy for. Thus, I have a perennial struggle between the vision in my mind's eye and the jumbly chaos that grows around me. The skill I have learnt over the last few years is to balance these two trains of thought and find a happy medium that works for our family and, better still, for the wildlife with which we share our home.

SMALL ACTS OF FAITH

If I haven't had time in the previous month, there are seeds to be sown in October. There are some vegetable seeds that can be sown under cover to provide winter and early spring harvests, but also there are flowers to be sown to provide colour the following year. There is a ritual to sowing seeds and each step is done purposefully and mindfully. From filling seed trays or pots with compost, smoothing it level, carefully tipping a few seeds into the palm of my hand and placing them carefully onto the surface of the compost, covering the seeds with more compost or grit and writing a label, to placing the filled tray or pot into a tray of water. They are all small acts of faith. A belief in nature's ability to do its part in the process and my hope that next year's garden will be abundant. I rarely sow seeds in a hurry. I take my time and enjoy the gentleness of the process: just me, the seeds and the sounds of nature around me.

Autumn sowings of flowers like nigella, ammi, honesty and calendula (and many more) allow the

Herbaceous perennials usually grow outwards from the centre

Willow stems are chock-a-block full of hormones that encourage rapid root formation. Take young stems of willow, cut into short lengths about 3-5cm (½ to 1 inch) and place in a glass jar. Cover the willow pieces with water, put on a lid and shake the jar. Remove the lid to allow air flow and leave for 8-12 hours. It's worth replacing the lid and shaking a few times during the process to encourage the release of the growth hormone from the willow. Remember to remove the lid after shaking. Strain the liquid to remove all the stems. The resulting liquid is a rooting solution in which you dip the ends of the cuttings before pushing them into compost or soil. Or, you can place the cuttings in the solution and leave them in the container for two or three weeks until roots have formed.

Alternative methods for making the rooting solution include using a blender to create a larger surface area of willow or to use boiling water over the crushed willow stems (in which case, do not use a glass jar).

> So often, gardening is not about instant impact, but about the longer-term relationship we build with our environment and all of its inhabitants.

> There are two times of the year to divide these perennials, autumn and spring. As a general rule, if a plant flowers before June, lift and divide it in autumn. If it flowers after June, a spring division is better.

seeds to develop into young, strong plants, which then almost stop growing during the coldest months. As soon as spring arrives, they can romp away and flourish in the summer sunshine.

It's also a good time to lift and divide herbaceous perennials. I particularly enjoy this process, partly because I think it's incredibly clever that nature can so quickly create new clumps of flowers from small offsets, but mostly because these are plants for free! Herbaceous perennials usually grow outwards and over time the centre may die off, leaving younger, stronger growth around the outer edges. This process neatly spaces the new plants apart from each other and gives them room to develop into mature plants. We can mimic this process by digging up a clump of roots and separating the growth on the outer edges to replant in a new position. Sometimes the process of division seems brutal: a spade is needed to chop through the root ball to divide it. With other species, it is less dramatic and small pieces can be teased away with the fingers. This ability to exponentially increase your plant stock is one of the things that I like so much about herbaceous perennials.

On the whole, I am often too busy in spring with other activities, so almost all division of herbaceous perennials is done in autumn.

At our new site, I am eager to create a large ornamental and cut-flower garden. A colourful space filled with different shapes and patterns all summer and then in the winter, swaying grasses and seed heads. I want to provide food and nesting materials for birds, hiding places for small mammals and insects. I want to encourage a diversity of animals, pollinators, predators and their predators into the space. I want to restore some balance in this space that has been over-grazed for so many years. My intention is to experiment with plants to discover which will survive the onslaught of the local rabbit population, because although I will put up rabbit fencing, in the long term, it would be better to create a garden that works with and around the wildlife that lived here long before we arrived.

I have purchased young herbaceous perennials, grown on in pots until their planting place is ready, and those that grow without too much damage from the wildlife will be lifted and divided to form much larger drifts of plants as the years progress. Ideally, I would be able to purchase enough plants immediately to have great visual impact in the new garden, but on the other hand, the pleasure I get from the slower development of a garden would be taken away. I revel in the unfolding of a dramatic floral scene and an instant quick-fix mass planting would deny me that pleasure.

HARDWOOD CUTTINGS

Autumn is a good time to take hardwood cuttings. Cuttings will produce a plant that is genetically identical to the specimen it is taken from, so it's worth choosing the strongest, most productive plants from which to take cuttings. Cuttings taken in October have time to slowly develop new roots over the winter, without the stress of needing to produce lots of leaves to photosynthesise and support the plant's growth above ground. This slow growth over the long period of the cooler months usually produces strong root systems and large healthy plants in the next year.

Sometimes I take the trouble of filling pots with compost for hardwood cuttings, but pushing cuttings directly into the soil works just as well. Labelling the sticks in the ground is good practice. If I don't label them at the time, I invariably forget what the cuttings are taken from and have to wait until they have grown, and possibly until they have flowered, before I can identify them.

It is easy to think that the cuttings aren't doing anything, but all the action is happening below soil level until the light and warmth of spring triggers the new plant to produce new shoots and leaf growth.

If I have remembered to take a tub of rooting powder into the garden, I use it, otherwise I just push the cuttings into the soil and wait. An alternative to bought-in rooting powder is to make your own root stimulating solution.

OVERWINTERING ALLIUMS

October is a good time to start planting overwintering onion sets. These are basically baby onions that have been paused in their growth and will continue to grow once they are replanted in soil. I prefer a variety called Senshyu Yellow, which grows into good sized onions, stores fairly well and provides a good strength of onion-flavour in meals.

I also plant garlic. We grow several varieties of garlic, not because I can noticeably tell the difference in the varieties in the kitchen, but more to act as a safeguard. Should one variety fail to thrive, a different variety may fare better. Varieties regularly grown in our garden include Messidrome, Solent Wight and Germidour, and are all autumn sown garlic. As a further safeguard, I also plant one or two varieties in the spring. I prefer softneck garlic for its longer storing quality. We use a lot of alliums in the kitchen, onions, garlic, leeks and elephant garlic – almost all of our meals will include at least one of these.

Most books that I've read advise to plant garlic with the growing tip at surface level, but I prefer to plant them much deeper, with a couple of inches of soil above the tip of a clove of garlic. The advantage of this is that as the roots grow, they often push the clove upwards so that more of it shows above the soil. The young shoots are attractive to birds like magpies and crows and before too long, your careful planting of garlic can be scattered across the garden. My more deeply planted garlic has time to establish a stronger root system, anchoring it into the ground, before the growing tips appear. Hence, they are more difficult for birds to pull up and I find most of my planting stays where it should.

Garlic can also be grown as a perennial vegetable. In the past when I have forgotten to harvest all of the garlic planted in the previous autumn, it has sprung into growth again the following year. The fresh green leaves can be cut and used in the same way as spring onions / scallions. I have also harvested clumps of immature cloves; removing the roots and basal plates and using them whole in casseroles, or chopped and used in the same way as a mature garlic. They have a slightly gentler, milder taste than cloves that have grown into large bulbs and stored for use. Growing garlic as a perennial vegetable is ideal if you want to use it as a companion for plants like roses.

DUCKS IN THE GARDEN

Towards the end of October, I give the ducks access to the vegetable garden. The bulk of the most tender vegetables have been harvested and the brassicas are netted, so our food is, for the most part, protected from the eager bills of a dozen dibbling ducks. My thinking behind letting the ducks have free access to the vegetable garden area is that they will spend their days rooting through the pathways and the beds finding tasty morsels. Mostly, I hope that they will gorge themselves on slugs and snails. The weather is often damp, encouraging the slugs and snails to the surface of the soil and it's not yet cold enough for the slugs to travel deep into the soil to hide. A couple of months of daily attention from the ducks has seen great results in reducing the amount of damage done to vegetables in the beds. Or at least, that's what I think.

In recent years, this has also been the time that I assess the available housing for our poultry. In Monmouthshire, that included giving all the housing and areas under cover a deep clean. All the used bedding was mucked out of the deep bedding systems and replaced with fresh new bedding and where needed, small repairs were made to the chicken wire and pallet walls or overhead netting. It seems that increasingly, as poultry keepers in the UK, we are being ordered to keep the birds under-cover and away from wild birds for months on end in the autumn and winter. This is a response to outbreaks of Avian Influenza and includes all poultry, even those kept as pets.

At our new site, we created a covered space in a block-built barn with a leaky roof, which we call The Lower Barn. There is plenty of room for the ducks to waddle around and, after four full days of working on it, Dave the Hero and I had made it secure from entry by wild birds, fox-proof (we hoped) and installed a new shed in it for the ducks to be safely locked away at night. The Lower Barn is tucked into the hillside on the south and has a tall hedge close to it on the north and east sides. Although it has some natural light filtering through the entrances and window spaces, they have been covered with netting and it's a rather dark and gloomy space. Fortunately, there was already a power supply to the building and several light fittings installed. Autumn of 2021 saw the most cases of Avian Influenza in recent years and we were instructed to keep birds inside and apply additional bio-security measures from the end of November – it was going to be a long and tedious winter for the ducks! When the ducks were eventually permitted to venture outside, it was the start of May and the garden had missed a full five months of slug patrol.

The main advantage of the autumn deep clean of the poultry houses is the increased material that is available for the compost heap and to use as a mulch on beds.

Used duck bedding is mild and can be put straight onto the growing beds as a mulch for the winter. As long as it isn't put on too thickly, it will break down well enough, or the worms will have incorporated it into the top layers of the soil, by late spring or early summer. Used chicken bedding is another matter. It's strong and 'hot' and could potentially damage the young stems of plants. It is advised to compost used chicken bedding for 12 months or more to allow it to mellow. I have found that it is fine to add to the compost heap as long as it is mixed in well and doesn't sit in thick layers.

COMPOST AND CONTAINERS

Almost every gardening book will have a section about compost and for good reason. Creating it is one of the simplest and most effective, enriching and empowering activities to carry out in your garden.

When we make compost, we mimic the process that occurs in nature on a constant basis all around us. Each year, deciduous plants drop their leaves during autumn and winter to replace them in spring with fresh, new growth. Animals drop their dung on the leaves, animals die and are covered by more fallen leaves. The remains of the small animals, dung and leaves are rained on, are trampled by wildlife and become hosts to a myriad of fungi and microbial life forms. They decay and break down and form a rich, nutrient dense food for the soil beneath and around the trees and shrubs. You only need to walk through woodland or forest or an area of land that has not been subjected to the heavy hands of over-enthusiastic humans, to find nature's own dark, rich layer of organic matter beneath your feet. Likewise, in fields and gardens, the manure of herbivores is broken down and returned to the soil by beetles, other insects and bacteria, providing a rich source of nutrients to the soil around the droppings.

CONTAINERS FOR COMPOST

Depending on the size of your garden or growing space, the style you like and your budget, compost containers can range from a designated spot in the garden that you place all your materials to make an open compost heap to a purchased wooden, multi-bay affair with roofed area or a hot composter. Containers can be made of plastic, wood, chicken wire or pallets, among many others; all designed to hold the materials in one place while nature breaks them down into compost. I have used different compost containers over the years and have been reasonably happy with them all. Nowadays I use either an open heap in the field or a bay made from four pallets strapped together to form an approximate square. This makes a compost heap large enough to make good compost without being so large that I am unable to deal with it if I want to turn it.

TOMATOES

From the time they are first ready to pick in late summer onwards, I harvest all the ripe tomatoes each day and take them to the kitchen to process, and October sees the start of the annual race to have ripened tomatoes before the first frost kicks in. Most years, I have to make a decision about whether to harvest the green tomatoes and take them into the house to finish ripening. But I delay that decision for as long as possible. Watching the weather and the blight alerts becomes a daily ritual. BlightWatch, and the updated version called BlightSpy, offer accurate information, based upon the Hutton Criteria, about the likelihood of late blight in your area. BlightWatch allows home gardeners to register for real time alerts when there is a chance that blight spores might affect their plants.

If I get a warning that blight is likely, I consider closing the doors to the polytunnel or greenhouse to reduce the chances of spores entering. But more than anything, I keep a close eye to see if the plants are infected and if so, I remove the leaves and take them out of the way. I also decide whether to harvest all the fruits on an infected plant to prevent the blight travelling into the tomatoes and spoiling them.

I have tried, repeatedly, to grow tomatoes in the open ground. There have been occasional successes where a plant has produced a handful of tomatoes before succumbing to blight. Because of this I have long since given up expecting a good crop from outdoor tomatoes and accept that I just don't have the knack of growing them successfully. Indoor grown tomatoes, on the other hand, are a different matter altogether!

Check to see whether your tomato varieties are determinate or indeterminate. You can pinch out the side shoots of indeterminate tomatoes, but if you do this to determinate varieties, you will drastically reduce the harvest.

The temptation to sow tomatoes early in the year is almost overwhelming. At a time when the skies are grey and the wind and rain feel relentless, I feel the call to sow seeds – to plant those tiny parcels of potential and to reaffirm my faith in the rhythm of the seasons. But unless you have a heated greenhouse, conservatory or other heated and light-filled space, there is little point in planting tomato seeds early. They will simply become tall, leggy plants that struggle to thrive. By waiting to sow until eight weeks before your expected last frost date, the plants can grow steadily and sturdily.

Mostly I grow indeterminate tomato varieties. These plants continue to grow taller and taller until the first autumn frosts arrive. Flowers and fruits are formed over a long period and the tomatoes ripen in succession. I like to try different varieties each year, but there are also some firm favourites that feature regularly. 'Moneymaker' and 'Gardener's Delight' have featured in my garden most years, partly from habit and partly because I know what to expect of them. 'Golden Sunrise' is a more recent addition to our tomato harvest, and the sweet yellow fruits are delicious.

To reduce the chances of blight killing the plants, the lower leaves are removed as the plant grows, allowing air to circulate around the stems. I'm also careful not to water the leaves of the plants, but to ensure that I water the soil around the stems instead.

It is advised to pinch out all the lateral growth that appears on indeterminate tomatoes. This means removing any of the little stems and leaves that grow where a leaf meets the main stem. It allows the plant to send all of its energy to making flowers and fruit.

On the whole, once these tomato plants have got to head height, which is usually around the same time as I am getting busier with harvesting and preserving food in the kitchen, I leave the side shoots to grow. I continue to remove the lower leaves and any very large leaves at the top that are blocking out light for the ripening fruits. This is not necessarily a good practice, but every year I feel the urge to allow the plants to produce as many fruits as it would want to. It rarely works out well. The plants often topple off their supports under the top-heavy weight of growth, and the plants expend their energy in producing green growth rather than more flowers and fruits and all I get is a jumble of tomato leaves to add to the compost heap. So why do it? It soothes my guilt at having removed all the lower leaves and making the plants into nothing more than tomato factories. It allows me to convince myself that I've let the plants grow in their natural pattern, even if it's only for a few weeks.

The only determinate tomatoes that I grow are a plum tomato variety called 'Roma'. These are bush tomatoes that don't need the side shoots pinching out. The fruits ripen almost at the same time, giving one or two (or a few more) harvesting days, rather than a continued supply over a period of weeks. I do remove some of the lower leaves, again to help increase airflow around the plants and reduce the chances of fungal infections.

Living in a damp climate has many advantages in terms of a steady natural water supply, but it does leave our cherished plants vulnerable to the diseases that flourish in moist environments.

CELERIAC

These creamy white, knobbly tubers, with a texture somewhere between rutabaga (swede) and parsnip seem to fall in and out of fashion in the culinary world. They have a mild celery taste and I like them in both stews and in a mixed root vegetable mash.

Seeds are sown in spring and planted out after all risk of frost has passed. The young plants need to be kept warm, otherwise they will start bolting (putting out flower stems in an attempt to produce seeds) if they get too cold. Celeriac is a moisture-loving plant, once planted out they should be watered into the ground well and a mulch applied to reduce evaporation.

Celeriac can be left in the ground during winter if they have some protection from freezing; a thick layer of straw for example. I have left them in the ground, but the taste becomes stronger the longer they

are left before harvesting. I prefer to have a more subtle flavour, so will lift them during the autumn and early winter and store them in the freezer, as pre-cooked mashed or in cubes.

WINTER SQUASH

I feel like I was a late arrival to the pumpkin party. Actually, I don't really like pumpkins. My memories of them are of the acrid smell of the burning flesh that filled the house at Halloween. I still find the taste of most of the large pumpkin varieties unpleasant and grow them only for the grandchildren to have the pleasure of carving one of Grandma's pumpkins at the end of October. However, other varieties of winter squash are a joy! Seeds sown in mid to late April will germinate and grow quickly into large, sturdy plants that can be planted out once the risk of frost is past.

Most winter squashes grow into large vines that can clamber up supports, holding themselves in place with curling tendrils, or they scramble along the ground, providing shade and smothering plants beneath them. This is not so good if you have food crops below the leaves, but is ideal for reducing weeds in the area.

I had been buying butternut squash from the greengrocer's shop for several years before I realised that I could be growing them at home. What a joy it is to discover that a particular much-loved plant will happily grow in our local climate; it feels like I've just been given a precious gift. Of all the winter squashes, I find butternut the most difficult to grow to a decent size. But as there are now only two of us at home, and Mr J is not a huge fan of squash, anything larger than tennis ball size is considered useful in the kitchen.

The delight of discovering a ripe squash nestled and hidden under an umbrella of squash plant leaves is almost overwhelming. It is exciting to watch a squash grow over the summer months, rapidly spreading out, covering large areas and the dark buttery yellow flowers attracting pollinators. Squashes have male and female flowers. The male flower stems are of an even size, whereas the female flowers, the ones that will become squashes, have a swollen part at the back of the flower. Seeing them develop is a pleasure, a sure sign that there will be squash to eat in the winter months. But finding a squash that you hadn't spotted growing is a bonus, an unexpected gift from nature.

A further joy of winter squashes is their storage ability. Once harvested the fruits can be left to cure.

Cure winter squash by keeping them in a dry, airy, frost-free place until the skins have hardened sufficiently that a thumbnail applied to the skin does not make a dent. They can then be stored in a cool room in the house for up to a year or more, depending on the conditions. Place the fruits so they are not touching each other and check regularly. If one shows signs of deterioration, remove it before mould spores spread to other fruits.

Over the next month or so the frost, wind and rain arrive in earnest and the huge leaves dry, crumple and disintegrate. I find something satisfying in seeing the process of these plants returning to the earth to feed and nourish another generation of plants.

What to sow in October

For sowing under cover

- ☐ Beet
- ☐ Calabrese
- ☐ Carrot
- ☐ Cauliflower
- ☐ Kale
- ☐ Spinach
- ☐ Spring cabbage
- ☐ Spring onion
- ☐ Winter lettuce and salad leaves

For sowing direct (outside)

- ☐ Autumn planted onion sets
- ☐ Fava bean | broad bean
- ☐ Field bean
- ☐ Garlic
- ☐ Mustards

For growing on the kitchen windowsill

- ☐ Basil
- ☐ Dill
- ☐ Parsley
- ☐ Beansprout
- ☐ Mustard and cress

NOVEMBER

As October gives way to November, the days are noticeably shorter. There's a cooler feel in the air and it seems to be the true start of autumn weather. As the leaves fall from the trees, the look and feel of the garden changes dramatically. Gone are the fresh and lush greens and blues of leaves on the trees against summery skies. The colours shift from overhead to beneath our feet, with yellows, reds and browns becoming dominant and skies becoming greyer and less bright. Over the cold weeks of November, as foliage dies down and areas of beds are put to sleep for the winter under a duvet of cosy mulch, the shape and outline of the garden becomes more obvious, highlighted by white frost sparkling in the weak morning sun. I start to look at the structure and infrastructure, assessing whether repairs will need to be done and for any changes I'd like to make. The winter months are ideal for making any additions to or change of the raised beds, supports for climbers, fences, gates and any other structures in the garden. There is no urgency to get repairs done and they can be carried out between rain showers, storms and spells of snowy weather.

I rather like November. Even though my body is very definitely slowing down, and despite being tired from two months of frantic work in the kitchen, I still have an energy, a buzz of excitement about the garden and an eagerness to spend time outside.

FALLEN, BUT NOT FORGOTTEN

Leaves can be left on the ground, where they will break down and feed the soil or you can gather the leaves and use them to create leaf mould. I used to gather them in heaps in readiness to create leaf mould in a large pallet frame, but our chickens had other ideas. They would run, skip and jump into the piles of leaves. At first, I thought they were doing so in order to find grubs, insects and those other bits and pieces that chickens seem to be able to spot. But the more I watched them playing in the leaves, the more I am convinced that this jumping onto the piles of leaves is done for sheer pleasure. Whatever their reasons, it made me pause or sit quietly to watch their activities. When, in late 2019, we decided

not to keep chickens for a while, this was one of my few regrets about that decision. I would miss seeing the chickens revel in Nature's playground.

Leaves gathered and left in a heap to break down, form wonderfully light and fine organic matter. Just like the floor of a woodland, it is dark and soft underfoot and has the potential to hold a great deal of water. Leaf mould is ideal for mulching borders and beds or for mixing with homemade compost to use in pots and seeds trays. I have made leaf mould every year for almost as long as I can remember, but I am really not very good at remembering to then use it at a later date, so it can be three or four years before I take a wheelbarrow to

the leaf mould pile to extract this natural resource for use in the garden.

As an alternative to making a pile of leaves to create leaf mould, they could be placed directly onto garden beds to break down over the coming months. This is ideal if you live in an area that isn't windy, but as yet, I haven't discovered many places in the UK that don't enjoy a steady flow of wind. And it seems that we choose to live in particularly windy sites! The constant coastal winds that we 'enjoyed' in Monmouthshire have been replaced on our new site by hilltop winds. Perhaps I should have thought more carefully about this before selecting this smallholding and perhaps I should have realised, considering there are wind turbines all around us,

albeit on the other side of the hills, that this site was likely to be subject to the same winds that drive the turbines. I learnt in Monmouthshire that wind isn't necessarily an issue in a garden. With careful choices and some judiciously placed windbreak hedges, there can be some advantages to a constantly replenishing air supply. Fungal infections and moulds are less likely to attack plants when there is a consistent flow of fresh air, and wind pollinated plants, like sweetcorn, thrive and seeds carried on the wind disperse over a wide area. If the seeds are of plants that you want to have more of, then that's ideal. It's not so good for keeping weeds, like dandelions, in check!

LEAF MOULD

Leaf mould is made from fallen leaves. Leave them on your garden beds where they fall or gather and place them in a container such as a hoop of chicken wire or a large plastic bag with plenty of holes pierced in it (for drainage and air flow). Leaf mould is made through fungal action and is a slow gentle process. Once you have gathered the leaves, you need do nothing else to them for the next year or two. Do not be tempted to add other ingredients to the pile, or to turn it over or mix it around. When you do this, you change the nature of the leaf mould and the fungal action will be reduced. Fungus will slowly break down the leaves into a fine, dark material that is ideal for making a seed or potting soil or, as I prefer to do, to add to the garden as a mulch. There are some nutrients in leaf mould, but not as wide a variety as there will be in a homemade compost. Piles of leaves are ideal places for wildlife to hibernate. Be careful when moving leaves and leaf mould, check through it first to ensure you don't spear a sleeping hedgehog or family of small mice or shrews.

I know that some gardeners like to run over leaves with a lawn mower to chop them up, increasing the surface area in the leaf pile and speeding up the process of making leaf mould. I do not chop up the leaves because there is a risk of killing caterpillars or pupae of moths or butterflies and it is an added process of work in the garden, when I have plenty of other things that call for my time. Added to which, increasingly, I am conscious of costs at home and in the garden e.g., petrol or electricity for a mower will just add to the overall cost of gardening.

FORWARD PLANNING FOR FLOWERS

November is an ideal time to plant bulbs to flower next spring and summer. From little crocuses that provide dots of colour only a few inches high to towering lilies that fill the air with their heady scent, bulbs can be incredibly useful in the garden. Many of them will happily stay in situ and quietly multiply year after year, giving an increasingly colourful display. If, like ours, your garden is home to squirrels, you may need to find imaginative ways to protect some of the bulbs. Squirrels eat a protein rich diet and bulbs like tulips and crocus provide them with an instant snack or one that can be buried for later consumption. Encasing the bulbs in a protective cage of chicken wire can help, although it means that your garden has buried wire in it. That's not a problem if you are leaving the tulips to naturalise, but careful removal will be needed if replacing the bulbs on a regular basis.

For the first year in our new home, I grew a large number of bulbs in pots so I could plant them in their final places when those beds were ready for them. It gave me a head start and a practice that I wish I had done in our previous home. Every year I saw flowers on television, social media and in others' gardens and wished that I'd been organised enough to plant some in our own garden, but I never seemed to have the right spot ready for them at planting time. By using pots, I could choose the right places for them over a period of months and have healthy, stronger plants to put in the ground on my own time scale.

SHALLOTS AND ELEPHANT GARLIC

If I haven't already done so, I finish planting garlic, elephant garlic and shallots in November. It is this planting process that makes it feel like the next growing year starts in the autumn.

I'm not sure how I managed to get so far through my life without tasting elephant garlic. Was I absent on those learning days? I had heard of it, but never eaten it. But thanks to Erica (*Erica's Little Welsh Garden*) I have now grown it for the last four years and delight in using it in the kitchen. Elephant garlic is not actually garlic, it's a type of leek that forms a bulb divided into cloves. It has a mild taste that imparts a gentle garlic flavour to meals.

It's worth noting that elephant garlic can be very slow to show itself in the garden. I've been fooled several times into thinking that it had failed to thrive, only to find a few weeks later that it had sent up a healthy green shoot. Patience is definitely key to successful elephant garlic growing. As a bonus, should you forget to harvest the elephant garlic, it will merrily stay in the ground and then produce a wonderful globe of creamy-coloured flowers on a tall stalk, providing interest at around 1.2 metres (4 feet) high. I grew them in a mixed border, in between dahlias and red kales, blurring the lines between ornamental and productive gardening.

I think that shallots are underrated. I grow long shallots rather than round ones, varieties like Zebrune and Longor. I find them incredibly useful in the kitchen and like to add them whole (dried skin and ends removed) to casseroles and stews. Or, sliced lengthways, they can be slowly caramelised and used in place of onions on burgers and hotdogs and added to dishes like quiche and omelettes.

I prefer the milder taste of shallots in many dishes where there are delicate flavours that can easily become overpowered by onions. But what I like about them most is that I can plant one shallot and by the end of the growing season, they have multiplied into six, or even as many as nine new shallots. It feels as though they are good value for money and for the space they use in the garden. They occupy the ground from late autumn until late June or July, freeing the space just at the right moment to plant more vegetables.

I like to chop a clove of elephant garlic and add it to the boiling water when I cook pasta. It adds a mild hint of garlic to every mouthful of the meal.

In recent years I've also started interplanting sweetcorn between the onions and shallots when it is ready to go into the ground in early June. This gives a chance for the roots to establish between the alliums and then, when the shallots or onions are lifted, the sweetcorn roots have space to spread out and occupy more of the cleared ground.

When we first started keeping ducks, we quickly discovered that they are quite partial to tasty young onion and shallot leaves, nibbling them off completely when they had the chance. To protect the young growth, I usually net the shallot and onion beds, using a fine netting, as soon as they are planted to prevent them from being destroyed by the attention of eager bills. The advantage of covering the emerging growth is that it also prevents corvids, like magpies and crows, from pulling them out of the ground. The nets are removed in March or April, once the ducks are banned from free-ranging in the vegetable garden and, conveniently, at the point when I will soon want to inter-plant between the shallots or onions.

I often intercrop onions and shallots with carrots. This is ideal because the smell of the onions can confuse carrot root fly and, similarly, the smell of the carrots confuses onion fly. What a perfect cohabitation combination!

PARSNIPS

Following the first frosts of the year, I start to harvest parsnips. Their seeds were sown in the spring once the soil had warmed. My preferred way to decide exactly when to sow seeds is to watch what Nature is doing. Parsnips, left to go to seed in the previous year, will start to germinate in pathways and borders, growing only when the conditions in my garden are just right for them. And that's the perfect time to sow more seeds in the growing beds. Despite the packaging of my parsnip seeds giving instructions to sow them in March and April, my garden shows me that, all too often, I need to wait until as late as May. Parsnips are fairly unfussy plants, they grow away quietly without shouting for attention, and then, when most other vegetables have been harvested or are waiting for warmer weather to return, the parsnip comes into its own.

The reason to wait for a frost or two before harvesting is that the cold turns the starches in the roots into sugars, making the parsnips sweeter. The first parsnip harvest always feels special. There's no real way of telling how well they have grown until I start to lift them and I find joy in discovering that they have thrived and produced a long straight root or a short, but very wide root. Occasionally there is a parsnip harvest disaster, in which there are plenty of roots, but they are forked, twisted or tangled into a knotted ball or, worse still, very few roots have formed. Thankfully those harvests are few and far between, and generally parsnips are a trouble-free crop in our garden.

In our temperate climate, parsnips can be stored in the ground where they stay throughout the winter months, harvesting just the amount needed for any one meal. If the ground freezes for weeks at a time, parsnips can be lifted and stored in a box of damp sand in a cool place like a shed or garage.

If I harvest too many parsnips in error, I boil and mash them and freeze the parsnip mash for use at a later date. It is ideal as a replacement for mashed potato when stored potatoes are used up or your supplies are getting low. I prefer the taste of mashed parsnip in many dishes: shepherd's pie is a particular favourite.

Each year I leave some parsnip plants in the ground to grow for a second year. As the weather warms in spring, they start new growth and by summer have produced tall flower heads of hundreds of tiny yellow flowers that are incredibly attractive to hoverflies and other pollinators. Interestingly, I have found that they are also home to a large number of ladybird larvae; these are always welcome creatures in our garden. They eat vast quantities of aphids and other tiny pests. Whenever I see ladybird larvae, I feel that the support system has arrived in the garden to rescue plants that might otherwise succumb to the ravages of thousands of tiny aphids. The parsnip flower heads mature and become seeds, which I gather and save for use the next spring. It is better to sow fresh parsnip seed, germination rates fall after the first year.

A word of caution about handling parsnip plants. The leaves contain furanocoumarins, which are phototoxic chemicals, they can cause burn-like blisters on your skin when exposed to sunlight (phytophotodermatitis). Usually, by the time parsnips are harvested, we are likely to be wearing long sleeves, coats and gloves, but in the summer months, it is worth remembering to keep arms covered if hand-weeding a bed of parsnips. A similar reaction can be caused by other members of the Umbellifer family, like carrots.

A different plant and a different reaction, but I now only ever harvest strawberries when wearing long sleeves that are tucked into a pair of gloves. I find the minor scratches from the edges of strawberry leaves irritating and painful. Anything I can do to ensure that gardening remains a pleasure is worth the effort.

STRUCTURED CRITICISM

Late autumn is also a good time to look at structural issues. Often the stormiest of the winter weather hasn't started and there are enough dry days to attend to any issues with boundaries and buildings that need attention. And as fewer plants are climbing over supports, there is better access to the support structures should they need some TLC. My intentions are always to attend to issues that need attention in November; the reality is that I spot the issues at this time of year and then take months to properly address them – perhaps it's because I find this work rather boring.

The exciting stuff happens when new structures are installed. Fences, pergolas, sheds, outbuildings, greenhouses and polytunnels make such a visual impact, as well as practical contributions to the garden. They offer new opportunities for storage, but more interestingly, for growing a different range of plants or growing familiar plants in a different way.

Once we knew where we were moving to and how much space I had to create a new garden, I contacted Direct Plants, a company that I'd worked with previously. I asked them whether we could work on a design for a large open framework structure that could be used for growing climbing plants, in particular roses. We explored suitable sizes and the ideal space between upright supports and eventually agreed on a design that would work for what I wanted to do, and would also be structurally strong enough to withstand the potential weight of the plants and the force of the wind. It is placed at the centre of the food forest and has a selection of climbing roses planted on each side of it.

Over the next few years, the roses should grow up and over the arch tunnel providing a slight wind break, a good display of flowers, a fragrant place to walk and to sit and contemplate, and then plenty of rose hips to use in the kitchen for wine and jelly. The climbing plants will provide a home and food for insects and birds.

Until the roses cast heavy shade below the arch tunnel, I will grow runner beans on the inside of the structure using baler twine or bamboo canes fixed near the top of the arch and angled down towards the ground. This arrangement will allow for easy access to the beans for picking as I walk through the tunnel and because the structure is designed to stand up to the strong winds that rip across the land, the bean plants should stay upright.

One of the core permaculture design principles is stacking functions. Think of it as building in multi-tasking to the design of the garden or space in which you live or work. The rose arch provides a multitude of functions, separate, related and intertwined.

A QUICK LOOK AROUND

While out in the garden checking for damage or changes needed to structure, I also take time to observe and appreciate what surrounds me. In the warmer months, it is easy to just pause for a while, or find a place to perch, sit or lie down to watch the activity and listen to the sounds of the garden. As winter approaches, I find this harder to do. The ground is often wet or cold, the wind can be biting and temperatures are uninviting. But there is value in observing our gardens at this time of year. It is easier to see the layout, the gaps, the crowded places. We can see where wildlife has made tracks from repeated journeys back and forth across the garden and observe birds more easily than when they are hidden among the leafy greenery. My garden observation visits are usually shorter at this time of year, but the pleasure is no less intense. The sounds around the garden are clearer; traffic noise, dogs barking and neighbours' activities are more acutely noticed, but so too is the chitter-chatter of small birds, the laughing sound made by corvids or the haunting call of birds of prey. A handful of times I have been privileged to see a mole creating a molehill: I could see the

It is in the still and quiet moments that we get to see the amazing, real-life action thriller unfold around us.

ground around the molehill moving and the soil heap increasing as the animal carried out its tunnelling. Once I witnessed a mole emerging from its dark, underground home to explore the air above its tunnel. I hadn't ever thought about the sound they might produce, so was surprised when I heard a series of little mole squeaks. Observations like these don't happen when we rush from one place to the next.

The shapes and form of dead or dying plants stand out against the emptier garden and it becomes evident which plants our native birds rely upon for additional winter food. The aromas in the garden are different at this time of year from spring and summer; they are more earthy and mouldy, making any floral or fruit fragrances seem more precious.

There are days when the late autumn sunshine kisses away the morning mists to reveal almost clear blue skies and provide us with some much-welcomed warmth. These are the best days for gardening. It's not so hot that hard physical labour becomes uncomfortably sweaty, but warm enough to enjoy being outside for hours on end. These are also the days which are often followed by frosts. The cloudless skies do not hold the heat under a cushioning blanket of water vapour, but allow the warmth from the sun to disappear off higher into the skies and cold air to fill its place. The clear, sunny days of November are when I mulch semi-tender plants and tuck them under compost or straw duvets for the season ahead. In our garden, November is truly a month of stark change that heralds the approach of winter.

What to sow in November

For sowing under cover

- ☐ Cauliflower
- ☐ Corn salad | lamb's lettuce
- ☐ Mustard
- ☐ Pea (for pea shoots)
- ☐ Spring onion

For sowing outside direct into the ground

- ☐ Fava bean | broad bean
- ☐ Onion sets
- ☐ Garlic cloves

For the kitchen windowsill

- ☐ Basil
- ☐ Chive
- ☐ Dill
- ☐ Parsley

WINTER

Every year I dread winter's arrival and yet there are special moments of joy and beauty in this, as in every season. To date, I haven't learnt to remember those occasions with enough clarity to focus on how much pleasure they bring among the gloomy, dark days leading to and from the solstice, but I'm working on it. January and February are often colder than December, but because of the increased number of hours of daylight, I fool myself into assuming that the worst is behind us as soon as the winter solstice passes.

So much in the garden stops growing. Below 5°C (41°F) even the grass grinds to a halt in its relentless pursuit of being just a little bit longer than I'd like it to be. But below ground level, there is still activity and there are also a few flowers that appear to remind us that life goes on.

Flowers of shrubs like mahonia, *Coronilla valentina* subsp. *glauca*, witch hazel, winter jasmine, daphne and a few others provide a sweet-scented blast of joy to the senses among an otherwise seemingly unperfumed landscape. It's not that the garden is entirely unscented during the winter, but that the fragrances are less floral or they are blown away quickly by wind. Early bulbs push their leaves and flower stems skywards, albeit by just a few inches, and burst into bloom. The first snowdrops of the year remind me that it won't be too long before the grey, weak light strengthens and the garden will be filled with colour, lush growth and abundance once again.

In the kitchen, more of our meals are made from food preserved in the previous months. The frantic work of the autumn pays off as we feast on an array of tastes and textures. Although with the help of the greenhouse and polytunnel we can eat seasonal, fresh vegetables for much of the year, I am grateful that we have good methods of preserving food to provide variety on our home menu. Winter vases and floral decorations are filled with grasses, seed heads and evergreen foliage.

DECEMBER

I take so much pleasure in walking around the garden, gathering greenery to decorate the house for the winter festivities. At this time of year, I fully appreciate those evergreen plants that, in the height of summer, can appear dark and solid, almost oppressive. Once the leaves of deciduous trees are little more than a mush on the ground, the steadfastness of firs, holly, sweet bay, rosemary and others shines through. I make a wreath for the front door and also place branches and sprigs of scented plants above picture frames and on the mantel shelf above the fireplace.

With a little careful forethought, it is possible to gather reasonably large quantities of foliage and berries without stripping the trees that you are gathering them from. Taking all the greenery now will stunt the plants' growth over the coming years.

In addition to green branches, many seed heads and grasses can be used in decorations. I recall as a child, using dried teasel heads and pine cones to make decorations for both the Christmas tree and for table decorations. I think my parents did very well to keep a smiling face when presented with a margarine tub filled with teasel and pine cones doused with gold and silver spray paint. To make the sparkly decorations stand up, the tub was filled with powdered laundry detergent, which had been moistened to make a stiff paste. As the mixture dried out, it set hard. I suspect my mother had a cupboard that she hid such decorations in after they had been on display for a suitable length of time. I hope that she reused the detergent to clean some laundry, rather than just throwing it into the bin.

I still collect pine cones to use as decorations. Piled up in a bowl or displayed in a glass vase, they can look attractive. Rather than their colour being the star of the show, it is their shapes that shine.

Image courtesy of Geoff at Brimwood Farm

OCCASIONAL OCA

The tubers of oca are planted in spring and grow throughout the year with slightly fleshy leaves that remind me of a fat clover and to my mind, almost insignificant flowers. It's said that once the leaves have died back, the small, colourful and knobbly tubers underground start to plump up. After a couple of weeks of waiting, the tubers can be lifted and either stored or eaten. We were introduced to oca a few years ago and have mixed feelings about it. It can be eaten raw, grated into salads or boiled and mashed or roasted, and has a slightly lemon/apple/radish flavour. It is worth noting that the tubers can store underground, to some extent, but I think it is better to harvest towards the second week of December and store them in a cool, but not frosty place. Left on the surface of the soil, the tubers become mushy once frozen and thawed – I learnt this the hard way. Following our first year of growing oca, Mr J and I decided that we didn't really like the flavour enough to warrant the effort of harvesting, scrubbing and cooking the small tubers, but that hasn't stopped me from growing them. They are a useful back-up should our crops of other winter-harvested vegetables fail to thrive. I've recently read that oca tubers can be left on a sunny windowsill for a week or two after harvesting to reduce the oxalic acid content and therefore, sweeten them. I have yet to try this, but will do so for the next harvest and I look forward to tasting them to see if there is a difference.

Oca also has another quality that I like in the garden. The low-growing foliage is incredibly useful as ground cover, which is helpful in reducing weed growth, as it can quickly form an attractive green layer, growing to 15-25cm (6-10 inches) high. Tubers that were left undisturbed and unharvested in our mild climate often regrow the next year, offering increasingly dense ground cover.

BRUSSELS SPROUTS

I suspect Brussels sprouts receive one of two reactions: you either love them or hate them. Our household has a divided opinion. Sown in early spring, the small, round seeds grow rapidly into young plants that can be planted out once they have two to six true leaves and have been hardened off. I plant the young seedlings deeper than they have previously grown and firm the soil around them very well. This helps to stabilise them in the ground, preventing wind rock. It may be an old wives' tale or I may have misheard, but I think firming soil around the plants makes the leaves of the sprouts bunch more closely together and form tighter Brussels sprouts. I am more than happy for someone to tell me that this is utter nonsense, but I shall continue to firm in brassicas in this way, just in case it is true. Brussels sprouts, as with all brassicas, can be netted to help prevent cabbage white butterfly and cabbage moth from laying their eggs on the leaves. While the butterfly does no damage, the caterpillars have a voracious appetite and can strip entire leaves in a day.

It is possible to grow Brussels sprouts to harvest from October to April by carefully selecting varieties that mature early and late in the season, and by judicious timings of when you sow the seeds. There is something incredibly satisfying about harvesting homegrown Brussels sprouts for a Christmas meal. I'm a big fan of the humble sprout. I like them lightly cooked, in boiling water for just a few minutes and then tossed into a frying pan with some bacon or pancetta. Much to Mr J's chagrin, it has even been known for me to eat this tasty combination at breakfast. In addition to the tight sprouts that grow around the stem, the tops of Brussels sprout plants can be harvested and used as a tasty alternative to sprouts or cabbage. Brassicas can be left in the ground until you need the space for another crop. The plants will form sulphur yellow flowers that provide an attractive display and a food for flying insects early in the year when there are fewer flowers available to forage.

FULL CIRCLE

Wherever vegetation grows you are likely to find some sort of living creature that might be classed as a pest. Pests will eat or damage the plant you are growing for food or for pleasure. For several decades we, as gardeners, have been offered an alarming array of lotions and potions, pills and drenches to kill almost any living creature that might appear in the garden. While this might seem like a good idea, there are also environmental and health impacts of using such chemical treatments in our gardens and on our food. Treatments that were once hailed as marvellous have been found to be detrimental to our health and to the world around us and have subsequently been withdrawn from use; there are still heated arguments about the safety of many products on the garden centre and shop shelves today.

There is another way to deal with the pests that visit our gardens: working with nature, growing organically and encouraging the natural predators of those pests. By providing the right environment for the pests' predators, nature will find a balance and do the pest control work for us. It's cheaper, less work in the long run and better for the environment and, therefore, our health.

There are some sprays and additives that are approved for use in an organic garden, but I still have concerns about their use. Here's my thinking – if a substance is used on or around a plant that kills the pest or renders it unable to reproduce, what impact does it have on the overall wildlife population and on us? If we continue to reduce the pollinator population and the population of other insects, what will the larger wildlife visitors to our gardens have left to eat? What is the point in installing a hedgehog house in the corner of our garden to encourage these lovely animals, if we then use slug pellets or other substances that reduce the availability of food for hedgehogs?

The impact humans have on their environment was demonstrated so clearly in 2020, during the lockdowns of the COVID-19 pandemic. Within two or three weeks of us staying at home and indoors, wildlife started to return to our towns and gardens in numbers that most of us haven't seen for some time (or possibly ever before). The news bulletins and newspapers ran stories of goats, sheep, squirrels and a myriad of other wildlife reclaiming the spaces from which humans usually force them by our presence and our activities. If I wasn't 100% convinced about my desire to work with nature rather than against it before, witnessing the re-emergence and resurgence of wildlife during those weeks of lockdown confirmed to me just how vital it is that we try to mitigate some of the effects we have on the life around us. Across the world there are working examples of how, when nature is given a chance to find its balance in our gardens and farms, pests are dealt with by predators and plants which not only survive, but thrive.

During our first year in Monmouthshire, the pests seemed to heavily outweigh the predators. Broad beans looked awful covered in blackfly, caterpillars devoured our cabbages and kale and slugs treated the tender lettuces as an all-you-can-eat buffet.

During the second year, it became obvious that more predators were moving in to feast on the pests and their predators were arriving too. As a wider range of wildlife flourished, even more predators arrived. There were times when I wandered through the food forest and became covered in tiny flying bugs (possibly beetles), at other times the ant

population would make themselves known as they hurriedly went about their business racing over and around my boots as I worked. Frequently I would sit on the sofa in the evenings and become aware of a bright green caterpillar walking on my clothes or, slightly more disconcertingly, appearing to be partying in my hair! Our fifth growing season was filled with the sound of wild bird song and the rustling of their movements among the trees, tall grasses and areas left to grow wild. Hedgehogs, toads, frogs, moles, bats made frequent appearances and I was increasingly aware that, when in the garden, I was never alone.

In our new home in Carmarthenshire, the balance of wildlife is very different. For years the land had been used for equestrian purposes; the grasses and broadleaf wild plants were razed to the ground on a continuous basis. There are several areas where stinging nettles and dock leaves thrive. The hedgerows are mature hedging trees which are home to squirrels and the scrubby undergrowth of these hedges are ideal places for the seemingly very healthy rabbit population. Likewise, there are plenty of slugs and snails in the damp ditches that surround each field.

During our first year, I left the grasses and broadleaf plants to grow unchecked in the fields. This was partly to see what grows on the land, but mostly because we hadn't, as yet, bought a suitable machine to mow the fields. Within a few weeks, we saw wildflowers, grasses and leafy plants flourish and with them an influx of pollinators like hoverflies, bees and wasps. This confirmed, yet again, that if you allow Nature to flourish, it will.

ADDITIONAL NOURISHMENT

The run up (or is it a countdown?) to the winter solstice keeps me going throughout December. The enforced jollity of the 'Season Greetings' compound the feeling of being overwhelmed by the short number of daylight hours, the weaker sunlight and the reduced amount of time I spend outside, but it's not all negative.

I see winter as an opportunity to rest and recuperate, to replenish our energy levels and to reset the rhythm of our bodies. In the days before electricity powered our lights and brought added daytime into our homes in the darkest depths of winter, we rested. While I wouldn't want to be without the modern conveniences that electricity brings to our lives, I feel that in many ways we have become a slave to a system that dictates how we should be equally productive all year round.

Just as a farmer might tend his animals during winter, providing additional shelter and feed to see them through the period when grazing is limited, we can tend and care for ourselves. The very fact that we block out 'me time' in our busy diaries, tells me that we are not caring for ourselves adequately on a day-to-day or regular enough basis. Taking inspiration from nature and my own body's reluctance to do much physical activity in the winter months, I allow myself to rest, repair and rejuvenate in readiness for another busy growing year ahead.

While I am resting more physically, I use the time to nourish my brain. Evaluating, learning, planning, imagining, wishing, dreaming can all be done in the relative quiet of the winter. This mental preparation means that as the temperatures warm the soil and plants burst into new leaf, I am already focussed on what I'd like to grow in the garden. I start spring with new ideas and an understanding of how to work with Nature to achieve what I'd like for the months ahead.

However, the winter months aren't entirely sedentary, there are still tasks that can be tackled and foods to harvest.

TAKING STOCK

During December, Mr J and I assess the year on our homestead; what we liked and didn't like, plants that grew better than expected and those that didn't, plants that we want more of in the following year and those that I won't bother growing again. We also look at the changes we've made in our home and the outbuildings, the livestock and our work/homelife balance. This in-depth scrutiny of every aspect of our lives has the potential to be negative and confidence bashing. But, as the solstice approaches, we have learnt that it is a time to be kind to ourselves and to celebrate another year of achievements and of learning. The process of regular reassessment enables us to adapt and change what we grow or where and how we grow it, to meet our ever-changing needs and aspirations.

This is also the month when I carry out a physical stocktake of all the food we have stored away. It is easy to make preserves, jams and jellies that end up pushed to the back of the shelves and forgotten about. By checking through all the food that we have put up for later use, I am reminded that we have them and need to use them. I also empty the contents of the freezers to see what is lurking in the bottom of them. There are likely to be foodstuffs that we don't like very much or had a huge glut of and shoved in the freezer 'just in case we need them'. Forgotten food is potentially wasted food, so I make some tough decisions about whether we are likely to eat them in the near future or whether they would be better to add to the compost heap and create space in the freezer for food that we will eat before it has freezer burn. The inventory of the freezer also helps me understand which foods to grow more of the next year and which plants to grow less of or to leave from the garden entirely.

PLANTING RASPBERRIES

If the ground is neither frozen or waterlogged, December is a good time to plant bare root raspberry canes. I prefer autumn fruiting rasp-berries as they require little attention for most of the year, pruning is very straightforward and the fruits can be harvested over several months. Bare root plants can be planted into a small hole in the soil and firmed in well. I usually plant them about 5cm (2 inches) deeper than the previous soil line on the plants. This helps them to anchor into the ground, prevents wind rock and encourages them to send out plenty of new growth in the spring. Winter care of existing autumn-fruiting raspberry plants is simply a matter of cutting all the stems back almost to ground level and applying a thin mulch of compost to feed the soil.

Raspberry plants will spread rapidly and in a small garden can become a nuisance. You can either cut them back in winter, or wait until the first signs of new growth in the spring. Alternatively, you can either cut back to around knee height or even leave the plants to grow new shoots on the existing growth. This will usually give you slightly earlier harvests, but the fruits may also be at or above head-height – worth considering if you have difficulty reaching up to harvest fruits or if the location of the plants would cast shade over sun-loving plants in the rest of your garden. If space is limited, it may be worth growing them in pots to prevent them running riot through your productive garden. If you have plenty of space, raspberries can be grown as a hedge.

MAKING THE BEDS

I rather like the look of the neat edges that raised beds provide. If you garden in an area that is prone to being waterlogged or flooding, raising the plants out of the natural soil level helps to keep them out of the water. There are a few plants that revel in having their roots constantly in water, but for many it will cause the roots to rot and the plant to die.

Equally, if you want to grow plants that like a particular type of soil, more acid or alkaline than your garden soil, a raised bed allows you to provide just the right conditions. In Monmouthshire, I chose to use raised beds because the ground was so stony, filled with broken glass and the soil in poor condition. Now in Carmarthenshire, I'm using raised beds to lift the plants out of the very wet landscape in which we live.

December and January are ideal months to create new raised beds and to repair or replace old and damaged beds. There are plenty of raised bed kits on the market, but equally, they can be made quite easily from locally sourced, recycled materials. Pallet collars make an instant raised bed and can be stacked to create deeper beds if required. Recycled timber, like scaffolding boards or wood from dismantled pallets, can be used to great effect. Railway sleepers offer chunky, solid sides to a raised bed, but care needs to be taken that they haven't been treated with chemicals that will prove toxic to the soil life and plants.

I found some decking boards on a structure that I wanted to repurpose. The decking boards created a good size bed and, because our new site is on a slope, I used fencing rails to create one side and the rails with decking boards on the top for the other side.

When the heavy rains started in January, I found that the depth of the beds still wasn't adequate to lift the plants out of the water completely. I imagine that it will be another year or two before I add extra height to the beds, because I will need to source some more reclaimed timber.

WINTER POTATOES

There is the potential to have a small harvest of new potatoes in mid to late December. The best seed potatoes to plant for a winter harvest are early varieties, those that in spring would take about seventy days to reach maturity. As the daylight hours lessen and temperatures lower, the rate at which plants grow slows down, and as such it takes more days for the potatoes to reach maturity. August planted seed potatoes usually provide a harvest in early winter. Place three or four seed potatoes in a 30 litre bucket or tub and cover with compost. You can either fill the bucket nearly to the top with compost (allowing enough room for watering) or just cover the seed potatoes with compost and then add in more as the plants grow. Either method should work and, if like me, you are likely to forget to add more compost at a later date, filling the container at the outset is a safer bet.

Once there is a threat of frost, the containers need to be taken inside and covered to protect them and to reduce the risk of frost damage – usually in a greenhouse, polytunnel, the porch of the house or even a conservatory. The plants can be wrapped with hessian, netting or horticultural fleece (my least favoured option) to help protect from low temperatures, but coverings need to be removed again during the day if temperatures rise, to ensure that the plants don't 'cook' in the heat inside the covering. It may seem like a lot of bother, but having freshly harvested potatoes on the plate for mid-winter celebrations feels very special and I think is worth the effort.

GROWING CHAMPIONS – ONIONS FROM SEED

Not long before the turn of the century, I was told by Ray, an old gardening friend (longstanding and more senior than I), that to grow superb onions from seeds, they needed to be sown the day after Christmas. After the hubbub and noise of a family Christmas Day, it seems an ideal time to head to a quiet space, on your own and gently and lovingly place seeds on the surface of moist compost. I suspect the timing has far more to do with seeking solitude than the number of daylight hours or any other factor that might be quoted. I'm fairly certain that onion farmers don't all rush out on December 26th to sow onion seeds for fear that their crops will be less than perfect!

Anyway, it was almost 20 years after Ray shared this gem of information with me that I first grew onions from seed, rather than onion sets. I didn't sow them at Christmas, in fact it was more like late February, but nonetheless I was extremely happy with the size and quality of the onions that grew from seed. I grew a variety called Bedfordshire Champion, which grew to the size of a tennis ball or larger and had a nice flavour.

Onions are another of those crops that leave me amazed by the cleverness of nature. From little seeds come grass-like leaves that within a few months grow and swell to form fist-sized onions. What an achievement, what a privilege to witness!

The onions I grow from seed seem to keep better than those grown from sets. It could be my imagination, but the onions I grow from seed seem to keep better than those grown from sets. Once again, I'm happy to take the credit for nature's work.

NOT ALL BROCCOLI IS GREEN

There are varieties of sprouting broccoli that are ready to harvest during December. Not to be confused with calabrese, which is the large, tight head of broccoli most often seen in supermarkets, sprouting broccoli has slimmer flower heads, but a multitude of them. The central floret is harvested first, prompting new florets to sprout around the stem. When those are picked, yet more will grow, albeit usually shorter in stem. There are green, white and purple sprouting broccoli varieties, and my preferred is the purple form. It's incredibly easy to grow, is a tough plant and produces tasty florets at a time of year when there is less available to harvest fresh from the garden. If left to mature, the flowers open in a riot of yellow hues and can, should you wish,

be eaten. When purple sprouting is cooked, it usually loses the purple colouring, leaving the cooking water distinctly purple-brown and the broccoli a rich deep green.

I grow varieties that produce their first flower heads in January or February, but there have been years when the weather conditions have brought that harvesting period forward to December. Harvesting can continue for several weeks as long as none of the florets are allowed to mature, open their flowers and produce seeds. If, for some reason, you are unable to harvest from your sprouting broccoli plant before the flowers start to open, it is still worth removing them to promote new growth of fresh florets for the kitchen table.

Seeds are sown in March to April and planted out when there are four to six true leaves and hardened off. The young plants can be planted deeper than they were in the compost where they were sown. Firm the soil around the young plant, taking care not to crush the stem. This helps to prevent wind rock. Sprouting broccoli plants grow to 110cm (3 feet 6 inches) or more, with large leaves growing from the central stem. They are prone to falling

over in the high winds of autumn and winter, so the plants can be staked to support them. I do not stake sprouting broccoli plants and they inevitably tip over a little. As long as the roots are not dislodged from the soil, they continue to grow and to produce a harvest. The main risks of leaving them in a more horizontal position are that slugs and snails have better access to the leaves and a reduction in airflow around the stems of the plants could provide ideal conditions for fungal diseases to develop.

When I notice that the plants are leaning, I remove the lower leaves and those touching the soil. Any that are yellow or brown are added to the compost heap, the leaves that are still green are fed to the chickens or ducks, who seem to welcome a change to their diet.

Although I have frozen this harvest, I find the results disappointing. Thawed, sprouting broccoli stems are tougher than I'd like them to be and the florets tend to be mushy. This is one of the vegetables that we now only eat while it can be picked fresh from the plant. The harvests are often so abundant that, by the end of the picking season, we are grateful that it will be several months before we eat it again. And always, by the start of the next harvest we are itching to savour the taste of freshly picked sprouting broccoli once more. This, it seems to me, is the ideal way to enjoy vegetables.

What to sow in December

Because the light levels and temperature are low, I don't sow anything during December with the exception of onion seeds. However, I may have a rethink of this as I have seen the idea of sowing seeds onto cold or frozen ground, in preparation for them to germinate as soon as the ground and air warm sufficiently. Some seeds need a period of cold to trigger germination; others will stay dormant until all the correct conditions are met for successful germination and healthy growth. This is what happens in nature and we can mimic it in our gardens.

JANUARY

The New Year brings with it a renewed enthusiasm for many gardeners. In the UK, all over social media, in print and in video, I see people sowing seeds for the new growing year. The problem I have with sowing seeds so early is that those seedlings and young plants need to be tended and cared for and kept frost free for several months before they can be planted out into the garden. Inevitably by late March, there are countless photos and questions regarding leggy plants from new growers who have succumbed to the idea that we need to sow seeds very early in the year. I understand that desire to be productive. I understand the need to feel like we are doing something after a few months of being more sedentary in terms of gardening. However, doing something productive can sometimes be counterproductive. Surely it is better to use the time to appreciate the quieter months, rather than rush headlong into growing too soon, only to find that the spindly seedlings have failed and that you need to resow or re-plant later on?

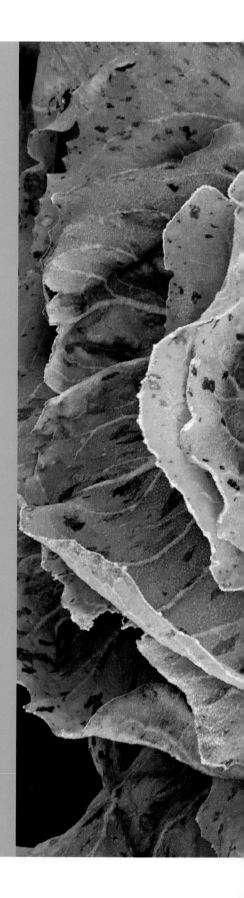

ARMCHAIR GARDENING

In a marketing frenzy, the seed catalogues start arriving in the post. I find it intensely irritating that in the age of instant access technology, what are no more than advertising manuals are printed and delivered to our homes. Yet another waste of resources. I dump them on the kitchen table on their way to the paper recycling bin. However, by breakfast time the next day, as I spoon oatmeal into my mouth, I find myself staring, through half-glazed eyes, at the brightly coloured pictures of 'super new salmon Busy Lizzie' and other such gaudy girls. I know I don't want to buy the plants, but with each spoonful of cereal, they become less hideous and more attractive. Thankfully, the catalogues are assigned to the recycling within a day or two and I am not tempted to make an order online.

It feels as though these printed booklets are a leftover habit, formed before the days of internet purchasing, when catalogues and mail order were the only way to buy seeds. I'm sure they serve a function and if nothing else, they encourage prospective purchasers to head to a keyboard and screen to order seeds and plants.

The rather useful result of their arrival is to prompt me to start dreaming about the spring and summer ahead. Just at the time when the light levels are low and the rain seems wetter than usual, I can escape into a fantasy garden where nothing eats my vegetables before we harvest them and the flowers all bloom perfectly at any given moment.

Seeds are a precious resource and wasting them, the nutrients they have taken from the soil, the water and space in the garden, is not a good thing.

WINTER LEAVES

There is something very special about being able to harvest salad leaves in the depths of winter. The first time I picked lamb's lettuce to accompany a Christmas lunch, I felt as though I had reached the status of 'real gardener'. I had braved the cold and fine layer of snow to make my way down the garden path to the glass barn cloches that had been protecting the precious salad plants during the autumn. I still remember the feeling of satisfaction and joy in gathering some lamb's lettuce and curled leaf parsley for our meal.

As a child, salads were something eaten only during the summer. They were light meals comprising butterhead lettuce, sliced cucumber and quartered tomatoes together with either sliced cold meat, a hard-boiled egg or grated cheese. The highlight of the meal was a few sultanas sprinkled over the plate. Occasionally, we had a potato salad

made from new potatoes and Heinz Salad Cream. Our family hadn't discovered the joy of mayonnaise or garlic and herb salad dressings, so salad cream or a basic oil and vinegar, sugar and mustard vinaigrette were used to add a little moisture to the plate.

Nowadays salads are an entirely different affair. With an array of different salad leaves, herbs and edible flowers, they offer an exciting range of tastes and textures. They include pulses and fruits, and salad dressings are homemade from oil and balsamic vinegar to which I add herbs, garlic and other seasonings or mayonnaise. I also make flavoured vinegars to provide further variety to the meals.

With careful selection of varieties and timely sowing of seeds, it is possible to grow a good selection of salad leaves throughout the year. And the time that I appreciate them the most is during winter. When most of our meals are 'hearty', some light, freshly picked leaves are a welcome contrast.

From loose head lettuces, like 'Winter Density' or 'Winter Imperial', to spicy mustard leaves and tasty pea shoots, many can be grown out in the open without much trouble. Growing them under the cover of a greenhouse or polytunnel allows them to grow faster, and for the slightly more tender varieties, to grow protected from the worst of the weather.

PALLET CRAFTS

January is a good time to attend to fences and other boundaries. Between the snow and rain that makes our country so lush and green, there are days that are crisp or dry enough to venture outside and get some repairs, replacements and construction work done. Pallet fences are quick and easy to make, and versatile in their uses.

A dismantled pallet offers an even wider range of potential uses. From making raised beds to creating signs for the garden or huge plant labels, the lengths of wood are usually even in size and easy to handle. To dismantle a pallet quickly and with the least amount of damage to the wood, I find a pallet breaker a useful tool. They are designed to lift the wooden slats away from the main frame of the pallet and then, with a bit of carefully applied brute force, the remainder of the pallet can be taken apart too.

I recently discovered that brightly coloured pallets, often painted blue or red, are the property of various companies and should not be kept, but returned to the companies for them to reuse time and again. I spotted a notification that they can be returned to the owner by contacting them online. I had found three blue pallets on our new site and duly completed an application for them to be collected by CHEP. It didn't take very long before a driver, with a suitably large vehicle, came to pick them up, free of charge and with a cheerful smile!

Pallets are also a great basis for making compost heaps or bays. With more than a little help from Dave, we built a composting compound. Fence posts that were a little too narrow to be useful for stock fencing were knocked into the ground, which allowed us to anchor some lengths of wood vertically and form a frame around three pallet compost bays. The eventual size of the structure was determined by the length of the wood that I had available. We created a frame for a roof and secured the side and internal pallets to the fence posts. In an ideal situation, we would have made this during the winter months in readiness for spring grass cutting, but creating this great compost-making space at any time of year is a bonus to my compost making efforts. We would have put pallets at the back of the structure as we made it, but I didn't have enough pallets and therefore, they will be added as we acquire more.

Not all pallets are equal and some should be avoided completely. Most pallets are treated to destroy any parasites or insects in the wood. Any pallet that is being sent internationally has to have a treatment stamp, which makes it easy for us as gardeners to identify which pallets are good to use in the garden and which are not.

Treatment marks can vary by country and the most common treatment marks in the UK are DB (debarked), HT (heat treated), KD (kiln dried), DH (dielectric heated) and MB (methyl bromide).

Pallets marked MB have been treated with a highly toxic pesticide and should not be used in the garden, not even to make compost bins, nor should they be burned on a fire.

RUTABAGA / SWEDES AND TURNIPS

Several root vegetables can be stored in the ground until needed in the kitchen. Swedes, known almost everywhere outside the UK as rutabaga or Swedish turnip, are useful vegetables that can be prepared in a number of ways. Sown in late spring, they grow steadily throughout the year and are ready to harvest from late autumn onwards. I use them as an alternative to potatoes and sometimes combine with potatoes to form a mixed vegetable mash or puree. Unless your site is regularly flooded or under deep snow for long spells, there is no need to harvest them all at once. Individual swedes can be harvested as needed and the remainder left to sit in the ground until a later date. When they start to regrow in the spring, the young leaves can be harvested for a tasty green to add to meals. I have a difficult relationship with swedes; I love the taste and texture of them, but I struggle to grow them to a decent size. Sadly, more often than not, the swedes are small and end up being very fiddly to prepare. I'm quietly hoping that swedes grown on our new site will be a better size.

Turnips are a relatively fast-growing crop. I sow turnip seeds in succession throughout late spring and late summer, preferring a white variety to golden or purple-top varieties. I harvest them throughout the growing season, prepare, cook and freeze them for use in the kitchen during the coldest months of the year. At a time of year when I have the least amount of energy for domestic chores, having pre-cooked food allows me to create tasty dishes with minimum effort. I usually add small pieces (and small portions) of turnip to casseroles and stews. Turnips are not glamorous vegetables, as a child, the only turnips I knew of were the ones featured in a book called *The Enormous Turnip*. But they are another useful crop that allows me to bulk out meals and eke out the meat we use per portion of food to provide an extra meal or two.

DEALING WITH FAILURE

For every gardener, every year something doesn't go as planned. I have never met someone who experienced a perfect growing year. Mr J would say that this is a good thing because if you reach perfection there is only one way to go from there. I'd quite like to experience near perfection in a garden, just to know what that feels like! But the reality is that between the sun and winds, rain and water table, the seeds, my interventions, the microbial life in the soil and hundreds of minute variations in the microclimate, local wildlife and many more influences, there is always something that could have grown better, produced a larger harvest or not succumbed to disease.

The potential garden space in our new home was exciting, but daunting. I could choose the size of the new vegetable garden and, in my imagination, I would tend 4.5 acres of well-manicured land. However, I learnt in Monmouthshire that I couldn't keep half an acre or so well-manicured, so there is no way that I could do that for even more space! It seemed the best way to start the vegetable garden was to create a space similar to the raised bed garden in our last home and, if necessary, expand from there.

The important thing is how we deal with the failures and what we can learn from them. Ensuring that we don't repeat a specific mistake is one step closer to getting it right!

CREATING A GROWING SPACE

Whether you are starting a new garden or regenerating an established one, the chances are that at some point you'll want to clear an area in which to grow plants, and that usually means assessing which plants you want to keep. Weeds are really just plants growing in a place where we don't want them. More often than not they are wildflowers and grasses, tiny tree saplings and young shrubs, but they can also be self-sown (volunteer) food crops or cultivated flowers.

At Byther Farm, we are creating a space where we work alongside nature, but all the same, there are plants in places where we don't want them to grow. For us, the use of weedkiller is not an option. A concoction of chemicals that can kill plants is not what we want for the soil, the soil life or for the pollinating insects that visit our garden, so we use alternative methods of weed control.

Like so many things in life, the preparation work is often the most time-consuming and potentially dull.

You could painstakingly remove all the weeds by hand and dispose of them, but that feels like unnecessary work when there are easier, possibly more effective and just as environmentally-kind options. My father once told me about his parents having 'daisy parties'. They were keen tennis players and were fortunate enough to have space for a lawn tennis court at their home. Each year they would hold a daisy party; friends would be invited for drinks and then, at an appropriate moment, everyone would head to the tennis court, get down on their hands and knees and systematically work their way across the tennis court, removing all the daisies and other weeds found growing in the grass!

Luckily, I have no such ideas for clearing every weed on our new site; far from it, I welcome many of the much-maligned self-sown plants because they are feeding the soil, bringing balance back to the land and supporting wildlife. But there are areas that we want to use that need clearing.

There are several ways to clear an area of weeds. The simplest, particularly for annual weeds, is to smother them and deprive them of light (and sometimes water) using a layer of material – sheet mulching. This can be as simple as a thick layer of cardboard or some plastic sheeting. I have used some damp-proof course membrane that was being sold off cheaply in a builder's merchant. Mindful of not wasting resources, I reuse it time and time again. I've also used a woven weed suppressing membrane, but don't think it's as effective as using a solid sheet of black plastic because it allows water to pass through the woven strands, potentially supporting the growth of some pernicious weed roots. Additionally, the woven material can shed strands of plastic that persist in the garden for years to come. In our garden in Monmouthshire, I discovered that birds had been using the strands of plastic in their nests. I found this fascinating and at the same time, heart-breaking.

If there is time to cover the soil and leave it for a few months, non-porous plastic sheeting will generally kill off most of the weeds; you may be left with some pernicious perennial weeds that will need their roots removing, but they will be weakened by the lack of light and water and their removal should be easier. The top growth and roots of annual weeds will compost in situ, returning organic matter and nutrients to the soil.

If you prefer a plastic-free garden, then a thick layer of cardboard over the area can work wonderfully. Several layers of cardboard (with all sticky tape removed) can be laid out flat and watered copiously.

Plastic debris woven into a bird's nest

Effort spent in preparing a growing space is, in the long run, a time saver. Far from seeing it as dull, it can be a great opportunity to get to know and understand the soil: the way the wind and water flows across your garden, which areas are shadier than others and whether you have frost pockets in certain points in your garden.

Plastic sheeting makes an effective sheet
mulch that can be reused many times

When the cardboard is saturated, it will soften and almost mould itself to the shape of the ground forming an almost (but not quite) impenetrable layer. Hold the cardboard down with bricks, stones, logs or lengths of wood. The cardboard will break down over time, but hopefully before then, you will have created the growing bed for your plants. When we don't have any cardboard available, we use paper feed sacks. They are the waste product from the poultry feed we buy for our chickens and ducks and are made from three or four layers of paper. Opened out and layered on top of each other, they work just as well as cardboard. If you have access to enough newspaper, a thick layer of that could work too. Layers of cardboard or paper can be added to continue to keep the area weed free until you are ready to plant in it. I've also used old wool carpet and cotton rugs for this purpose. I don't recommend the use of carpets with petroleum-based products for mulching. While they do an equally good job of smothering weeds, there is a potential for leaching of chemicals into the soil and if you choose to grow without the use of fossil fuel-based products, this may be counter-productive. They will also shed fine strands into the ground making a tangled mess of plastic and other petroleum-based fibres.

In recent years, plant-based sheet mulching has become available. These include rolls of paper designed to suppress weeds for a short time while your plants establish themselves or paper made from corn starches which are said to break down over a period of months or years, depending on the thickness of the material used. I tried a heavy-duty corn starch roll in our new food forest in Carmarthenshire. The sheet mulch was easy to unroll across an area and pin down to prevent wind getting underneath it and blowing it away.

BARE ROOT TREES

When setting up a large new site, creating a new garden or even adding a single tree to your garden can dramatically change the look, feel and growing environment. Buying trees in pots can be costly, and on the whole, bare root trees are a more economical way to purchase them, particularly if you are buying in large numbers. The ideal time for planting bare root trees and shrubs is from late November to March because once trees and shrubs have become dormant, they can be moved with less trauma to them. In Carmarthenshire, faced with acres of empty fields that I wanted to transform into a lush food forest, an agroforestry orchard and gardens surrounded by hedges, I knew that there was going to be a lot of planting of bare rooted trees, from tiny seedlings to large, three- or four-year-old trees. And equally a huge number of shrubs, both for fruits and flowers.

In our previous garden, I planted some trees that were 120-150cm (4-5 feet) tall and others of the same species that were no more than knee high. I planted the taller trees because I wanted some instant impact, but I found that the smaller trees, those that were one-year-old rather than two- or three-years-old, were quicker to establish and outgrew their larger companions. Lesson learned: bigger isn't always better.

The trees in the food forest and orchard have come from various sources. Some I had lifted from our previous home and tended for over a year in large tubs. Others were purchased locally, like some Welsh varieties of apple. Yet more have been bought in bulk or gifted by our friends at Direct Plants as bare root trees and planted with care. Although most of these trees will not provide a decent crop for a few years or more, their impact for local wildlife started almost as soon as they were planted by providing homes for insects, perching places for birds and by slowing the movement of the wind and water across the land.

A quick and easy way to plant bare root whips and saplings is to use a spade to cut a cross into the soil. Then make a third cut at a right angle to the cross and lever your spade downwards. This will open up the centre of the cross, allowing you to place the roots of the young tree into the ground. As you move the spade to the vertical position again, the soil will close around the roots and you simply need to firm it in using your boot.

My friend JB planting Lombardy poplar in our mixed species hedging

Scarlet kale works well in a mixed border

KALE

We are not huge fans of the taste of kale, but a few plants in the garden provide us with fresh leafy greens to cook for much of the year. In spring and summer, I grow rows of red Russian kale to cut the young leaves for use in salads.

I grow kale to include in vegetable boxes, for feeding to poultry, for adding a little to our meals, for colour and structure in the garden beds, but above all, I grow kale for the wildlife in our garden.

Grown in the open during the summer months, kale offers a place for cabbage white butterflies and cabbage moths to lay their eggs. In the late winter and early spring, as kale produces flowers, it provides food for pollinators and early forage for bees, while offering us a cheerful display of flowers held over the green leaves.

Kale seeds can be sown from early spring to early summer. My preferred varieties are taller growing ones that add a splash of colour and texture to the garden. Grown among ornamental plants or flowers intended for cutting, kales with bright purple ribs or with deep red leaves make a great contrast and foil for light and airy foliage and delicate flowers. A black kale, like Cavolo Nero with its long dark, crinkly leaves, makes an ideal backdrop for brightly coloured flowers like zinnia or dahlias.

It is during the winter months that kale really proves useful. It is generally hardy and will withstand most of the conditions that our wet and windy winters throw at them. The taller varieties often fall over in the wind, but as long as there are still some roots in the ground, I tend to leave them in the fallen position. It seems that the main stem being horizontal triggers the plant to grow additional shoots with even more leaves, more florets to harvest and, when the plants eventually start flowering, there are even more bright yellow flowers for pollinators to visit.

There is such a wide variety of forms of kale, that it is possible to have a slightly different taste of kale each day of the week, should you so choose!

TOOLS AND EQUIPMENT

Winter is the ideal time to check over equipment and tools, to do maintenance work and make repairs. It took me a long time to understand the importance of these mundane and often boring tasks. To start spring with tools that are well cared for and have been stored away appropriately is ideal and it means that you can carry out gardening activities without having to first repair the necessary kit.

Mr J and I are often slow to make purchases of large items of equipment. Rather than make a wrong decision about tools, we delay making purchases until we are comfortable with the choice we've made. We then try to make sure that we take the best care that we can of each piece. And so it took over a year to select a second hand ride-on mower to cut the grass at our new home.

When we finally took delivery of it (in September 2022), I was so excited. Maybe excited wasn't quite the right word; I was daunted, but determined to use it. I spent some time that day learning how to drive it and how to use the cutting deck and, when I got stuck, mentally not physically, I just turned off the engine and left the mower where it was until Mr J came home from work to watch, guide and encourage me to drive the mower down the hill into the flower field to continue cutting the grass. The next day, my confidence had grown a little and I headed into the food forest to ride up and down the hill, systematically cutting the grass between the rows of planting. I cut a strip of grass beneath the rose arch and then at the top of the hill turned, mowed along the top a little, turned again and mowed down the side of one growing bed. It looked superb and I was sure that I could continue in this pattern across the whole of the food forest. Confidence growing, I cut under the rose arch once again, this time guiding the cutting deck next to the raised bed and was delighted that all it needed was a quick pass by with the strimmer along the very edge of the raised bed for it to look neat and well-cared for. This was grass-cutting success.

The mower has rear wheel drive, which means that the back wheels turn before I see the effect at the front and I hadn't noticed that one back tyre had gone up and over the shallow edging of the raised bed. At the top of the hill, I steered to go around the corner and heard a peculiar noise coming from behind me. I turned the engine off and jumped down to see what the problem was. The rose arch is based on a polytunnel frame and to ensure the arches sit properly within the grounding poles,

they are secured with a 10cm (4 inch) nail, which is hammered down at an angle to form a sideways L shape. This secures the arch and prevents something accidentally snagging on the nail. Or it would do, if I had remembered to complete this stage of building the rose arch. And something was well and truly snagged on the nail now!

As the tyre deflated, so did my confidence, to be replaced with a big dose of humiliation. I telephoned the company that supplied the ride-on mower and admitted that I'd broken the machine less than 24 hours after delivery. They were very kind and although I'm sure they had a very good chuckle in their office, they didn't once laugh aloud at me. Lesson learnt from this episode; when I begin to feel I've mastered something, I need to stop and look around me carefully, because that's the point at which I'm very likely to be vincible. On the plus side, I found a name for the mower, Vince.

What to sow in January

Seeds to sow without heat

- ☐ Fava bean | broad bean
- ☐ Cabbage
- ☐ Carrot
- ☐ Cauliflower
- ☐ Corn salad | lamb's lettuce
- ☐ Kale
- ☐ Mustard leaves
- ☐ Pea

Seeds to sow with heat

- ☐ Aubergine
- ☐ Chilli and pepper
- ☐ Onion seeds
- ☐ Shallot seeds

FEBRUARY

Every year I forget that February, despite having the least number of days, can drag on for what feels like a very long time. Cold, grey, wet and windy, the weather is uninviting, but despite all of that, my desire to get on with things increases. I think of February as the last month of winter, the last few weeks to get through before a hint of spring arrives.

In the hedgerows and garden, snowdrops appear, holding their delicate petals aloft, even when that's only a few inches high. With the temperatures still cool enough to keep grass growth slow, the only thing that seems to grow is the size of the muddy patches created by the ducks.

UNDERSTAND YOUR PRIORITIES

In Monmouthshire, I spent three years slowly creating and developing the raised bed vegetable garden and the areas where we grew fruits. It was only after they were complete that I moved on to creating an ornamental garden, even though that also contained some edible plants. I had always felt like something was missing in that space and as soon as I put in some ornamental plants and flowers, I understood that they were what I needed to give the garden the feeling of home, peace and tranquillity.

Remembering the feeling of relief, of reduction in stress, of joy that I found once the ornamental plants were introduced, they were the first thing I planned for our new growing spaces. Gardening is a process of constant learning, of adjusting and evolving practices and this is a clear example of learning from experience and using that knowledge sensibly. The fruit trees were planted into the food forest and surrounded by ornamentals, herbs and fruiting shrubs and bushes. Our new raised bed vegetable garden was planted with perennial, biennial and annual flowers before any vegetables were planted. In part, the vegetable beds were a holding space for the ornamentals to grow and mature before being moved to the as yet blank field that was to become the flower garden. And in part, I wanted to enjoy every moment of being in the vegetable garden as quickly as possible.

Understanding how we respond to our immediate environment can help us to create a gardening space that is nurturing not just for the plants grown in it, but for our own well-being too.

I had also learnt that having an area under cover was ideal in our climate. Our new site had no covered growing space, so creating one was a priority.

Every year I say I am going to wait until March and April before sowing any seeds and for the most part, that is what I do. However, more often than not, during the last few days of February, I indulge my yearning for seed-sowing.

This task is not done in the greenhouse or polytunnel, but at the kitchen table. A bag of compost on the floor, a bin liner or newspaper spread out over the table and seed trays or modules appear and remain in situ until my urge to do some gardening is sated.

Polytunnels provide shelter from the wind and prevent contact with ice and snow, but they don't seem to hold warmth in the way that a glass greenhouse does. One solution is to create extra layers of protection and insulation within the polytunnel. Cold frames, barn cloches, even a simple frame made from canes with bubble-wrap pegged to it, can help to insulate a small area within the polytunnel in which you can grow a few plants. Having said all of that, a truly tender plant is unlikely to survive the freezing and near-freezing temperatures of the average winter in a polytunnel.

The problem with sowing seeds so early, is that they need a home of some kind until the weather permits them to be moved outside, to a spot under cover or into the ground. At our previous home, this wasn't really a problem. The kitchen was flooded with light all year round and there was a greenhouse 20 feet from the back door. The kitchen in our new home is dark and dingy and there is no greenhouse nearby. For our first year in Carmarthenshire, the tiny cottage windowsills were covered in trays and pots of plants.

A further way to improve the temperature under cover is to provide a source of warmth. A compost heap within the polytunnel will provide a low gentle heat as the contents decompose. Depending on the size of your polytunnel, you might want to create more than one compost heap at the end of the autumn, to provide some warmth in the cooler months. It is unlikely that a cold compost heap is going to heat your polytunnel very much, but the addition of thermal mass may help a little. You could also try large containers of water. Dark coloured containers filled with water and covered to prevent animals falling into it will absorb heat from the sun, however weak the sunlight seems, during the day and slowly release it at night. If possible, cover the opening with a fine mesh or netting to prevent flying insects laying eggs in the water.

LEEKS

By February, I have often used all of the bulb onions harvested in summer, and most of the frozen onion greens and it is too early for perennial onions to provide much of a harvest. This is the time that leeks become the allium stars of the garden. Although I have been harvesting them throughout the winter for use as a side dish or to add to soups and stews, now I harvest leeks to use as an onion substitute. Any dish that requires onions can have finely chopped leek instead.

In our temperate climate, leeks can be stored in the ground over winter and harvested as needed in the kitchen. To freeze, they can be sliced, blanched in boiling water, and cooled rapidly before freezing. Or they can be sliced and frozen without blanching. I prefer to prepare them fresh for each meal, as I find they have a slightly slimy texture once they have been defrosted.

Any leeks that are not used during the spring can be left in the ground to produce their dramatic seed heads. Each plant will send up a stalk that holds the globe-shaped flower head high above the leaves. Individual flowers are tiny, creamy-white and, depending on variety,

ENCOURAGE WILDLIFE

Making the change or starting to grow in tune with nature is a relatively simple affair, you just need to make the decision and commitment and then employ some simple ways to attract more pollinators and predators into your garden. There is a host of plants that will attract beneficial insects and by creating a place for the plants to grow (or planting them). It is possible to purchase some beneficial insects, (like ladybirds), but I choose not to do so because I am concerned that I will then create an imbalance of predators that don't have enough pests to thrive upon. Providing appropriate habitat for wildlife will also encourage it into your garden surprisingly quickly.

WILDLIFE PONDS

A small wildlife pond can be very simple: bury a washing up bowl in the ground so that the rim is level with or very slightly above the soil and put a stone in it to allow inhabitants to scramble in and out of the water. Fill the bowl with rainwater or, if you don't have any, just leave it, and the rains will fill it up before too long. I find it fascinating that pondlife will appear as if by magic in a relatively short space of time. Providing a few plants around the outside of the pond will give shelter to small animals visiting it.

BEE, BUG AND WILDLIFE HOTELS

Offering suitable places for insects as a refuge or place to live is a great idea, but they do need to be well researched, properly made and maintained carefully. A pile of sand in a sunny spot that has some cover from heavy rain can be a home to ground dwelling bees. I'm not convinced that large insect hotels are a good idea as they are unlikely to be able to offer all the different conditions that a variety of animal species would need in one place. Several smaller, specifically designed hotels might be more effective in supporting a range of insects and animals. Purpose-built houses can provide shelter to hedgehogs, but similarly, they need to be designed in such a way they won't give access to dogs or foxes and also that doesn't let them become soaked with rain and waterlogged during the winter.

WILDLIFE CORNERS

If space allows, leaving an area of your garden to grow wild is an ideal way to attract wildlife and support the population of some species. At Byther Farm we leave areas of stinging nettles, brambles and a host of other weeds to offer shelter and food for birds, butterflies and other wildlife.

In Monmouthshire, in many spots across our homestead this happened more by happy accident than by design. I designated a couple of areas that I would leave well alone and allow nature to take its course; it seems that between nature's amazing ability to reproduce and my lack of time, energy or attention, there were much larger areas than I had intended that became wildlife hotspots. The number and variety of species that moved in continued to surprise and delight us. In gardens where there isn't space to leave a patch to grow wild, it is often possible to recreate the wildlife areas using carefully curated versions, like growing a thornless blackberry rather than a prickly wild bramble, or making a leaf mould pile that hedgehogs can access.

might have a pale mauve hue. Most allium vegetables will produce these exquisite flowers.

I plant many alliums in the flower beds as dual-purpose plants. Some of the leaves can be harvested and then the plant is left to produce flowers. The added bonus being that the seeds can be collected for sowing the following year. It's worth selecting the most vigorous and healthy plants from which to collect the seeds; traits that you want in your leek plants for future generations.

Leek seeds are sown in February to March, they germinate readily and produce fine, grass-like seed leaves that often have the seeds still attached. They look to me as though they are carrying tiny beetles on the top of each plant, but on closer inspection, they are the seed casings.

Once the seedlings are hardened off, I plant them in the clumps or groups that they germinated in, into a holding bed to grow on for a few months. When the young leeks are around pencil thick, they are planted out individually in their final growing position. I do this by making a hole in the ground with a thick dibber, dropping the plant into the hole and watering it in. There is no need to refill the hole with soil, the water will gently wash some soil around the roots and the hole allows the leek to develop with minimum effort. Soil will fall down into the hole and surround the leek, blocking out the light and blanching the lower part of the plant.

HEDGE PLANTING

For the hedges, I ordered young hedging trees that were no more than rooted single stems, referred to as whips. It took hundreds of these little plants to form the hedgerows around the perimeters of the paddocks. They looked rather pathetic waving in the wind, but I knew from our experience in Monmouthshire that within a handful of years, the hedges would be over head-height, bushy and teeming with wildlife. For the east to west hedges that bordered our neighbour's field there is mixed hedging of plants that produce hips, haws, nuts and berries, while on the lower side of the slope next to The Runway, a hedge of hornbeam will act as a backdrop and windbreak. It's an investment, both financially and physically, but more than anything, it's an emotional investment in the future success of this site. Between paddocks, running north to south, I planted a hedge of currant bushes with plants I had brought with us: red, white and blackcurrants, together with josterberries and chuckleberries, they will form a productive and edible hedge to the food forest. I had been taking semi-ripe and hardwood cuttings of currants for three years, growing them in pots, ready to take with us when, eventually, we found a new home.

As long as the ground isn't frozen, hedge planting of dormant, bare root trees can continue throughout February and into March. I feel that a garden is never too new or too mature to benefit from a new hedge. They provide the backdrop, the structural outline, the framework for an area.

In most of the urban houses we have lived in, hedges have been of a single species and more often than not, had been left to grow too tall and wide for their allotted space or intended purpose. Hedges of fast-growing trees, like *Cupressus* x *leylandii*, planted to provide privacy, are left to grow for too long without attention. They can grow at an alarming rate, not only in height, but in width too.

Conifer hedge removed, showing how wide it had grown

Even in gardens where these huge trees are well-tended, I think they are just unsuitable for the confines of the average urban home. Added to this, they offer little in the way of support for wildlife, except a nesting place for a few birds each spring. There are slower growing hedging conifers, but they are less popular because who wants to wait ten years to block out an unsightly view or a nosey neighbour?

Choosing the right hedging plants for the garden is important because they are likely to be in your garden for years to come. They will impact upon almost everything else you plant, either by blocking the light or using nutrients and water, or by providing needed wind shelter or framing a garden.

And hedges aren't just tall plants, they can be low growing like lavender, rosemary, hypericum, box or roses. They can even be step-over fruiting hedges.

These are fruit trees on a specific root stock that have been trained to grow a few inches above the soil level, but nonetheless, flower and fruit. I think there is something rather unnatural-looking about these low-level trees; they look confined and stunted, but at the same time, I find them attractive and fascinating.

PRESERVES AND STOCK

The glut of any harvest is never wasted. In one way or another I use the surplus or share it with family, friends and neighbours. Fruit and vegetables that are not eaten fresh are stored or preserved in some way and if there is simply too much in the garden, they are fed to the animals. However, if the harvests have deteriorated beyond use, they are returned to the garden via the compost heap. Mr J and I do not much like pickled vegetables, preserved in spiced vinegar, but we do both like chutney and relishes. If I haven't had a chance to make them during the autumn, the winter months are a good time to gather ingredients from the freezer and storage areas and create rich and tasty relishes and chutneys.

I am not sure what the difference is between a chutney, relish, marmalade and sandwich pickle.

Increasingly, I am interested in hedges that can provide boundaries without blocking the view across the garden or casting too much shadow. Low growing hedges can add structure and a sense of formality, but they can also be productive, providing a harvest of flowers, fruits, hips or berries, whether they are consumed by us or by the local wildlife.

Perhaps they are all fairly similar and the name reflects the locality of the maker. Whatever they are called, I rather like a mixture of vegetables and fruits, chopped finely, with herbs or spices and preserved in vinegar and sugar. Mr J's favourite is an onion jam, which I make using onions that are likely to become too soft for use if they are stored. Chutneys are eaten with cold meats, cheese and bread or crackers and occasionally I include a healthy spoonful in a casserole, stew or stir-fry meal to add a richness and depth of flavour.

I also use surplus vegetables to make a rich stock that is later the basis of a meal. Having stock readily at hand is a useful time-saver. I do not use purchased stock cubes or granules because many of them contain gluten and are high in salt. By making my own stocks, I know exactly what has gone into them. Some vegetables are more useful in stocks than others. Celery and lovage add a depth of flavour to meals that I haven't found in other vegetables and carrots impart a sweetness without being overly sweet, like parsnips can be when used in stocks. I make two distinct types of stock; a clear stock and a thick stock. The clear stock is made by straining the liquid away from all the vegetables and the thick stock is made by keeping the vegetables in the liquid and pureeing it when it has cooled. The thick stock is ideal for making soups, stews and using as the base for a pie filling.

What to sow in February

Seeds to sow without heat

- ☐ Beet | beetroot
- ☐ Fava bean | broad bean
- ☐ Brussels sprout
- ☐ Carrot
- ☐ Cauliflower
- ☐ Salad leaves
- ☐ Spring onion
- ☐ Radish
- ☐ Kale
- ☐ Mustard leaves
- ☐ Pea | snowpea
- ☐ Spinach
- ☐ Turnip

Seeds to sow with heat

- ☐ Red cabbage
- ☐ Celeriac
- ☐ Celery
- ☐ Chilli and pepper
- ☐ Leek
- ☐ Onion seeds
- ☐ Shallot seeds
- ☐ Tomato (sow eight weeks before last frost date)

SPRING

This season brings a mixture of bright clear days followed by bitterly cold nights and blustery, rainy periods that batter the fresh growth in the garden. The wind seems relentless in its pursuit of flattening everything in its path as temperatures climb and plummet in equal measures. Over the last four to five decades, I have seen the change in the weather patterns. Changes that were predicted by scientists. In the temperate climate of Wales, 52° north, the weather seems wetter for longer and the storms harsher, more violent and capable of doing more structural damage than before. The way in which we garden has had to adapt in response to the shift in weather patterns.

As the number of daylight hours increases, so does my enthusiasm for being outside and for beginning the process of sowing seeds of annual vegetables. Spring flowers bring a welcome splash of colour in the garden and small green buds appear on early flowering trees. The transformation of the landscape begins and once again the focus moves from the ground to eye level and above.

In the vegetable garden, this is a busy period of sowing seeds, potting on, planting out, watering and caring for young plants and is a time filled with hope for a productive and abundant harvest in the months ahead.

By the end of spring, house martins and swifts have returned to nest in outbuildings and in nests that cling to the sides of the house, just under the eaves. Blossoms in the hedgerows have come (and in some cases are long gone) and grasses and wildflowers have grown rapidly, flowered and are casting their seeds for next year's plants.

This is the hungry gap: the period during which there are traditionally fewer fresh vegetables to harvest. The winter crops are mostly finished, but the new season's growth is not yet ready to take to the kitchen. However, with a little judicious planning, it is possible to have a plentiful supply of food to harvest, although choice is not as wide as later in the year.

MARCH

March is a month of predictably unpredictable weather. In some years, it brings a warm dry spell that fools me into believing summer is just around the corner, and in others it brings north winds and freezing storms that call for rich, warming casseroles and stewed fruit and custard. For the vegetable grower, March can be a busy month of filling seed trays or seed beds with compost and sowing seeds of the food we hope to harvest later in the year. One thing is certain though, for most young plants it is too early to plant them out into the garden.

Harvest rhubarb by pulling the stems away from the base. Do not cut the stems as this can leave the plant susceptible to infection. Stop harvesting rhubarb by the end of July to allow the plants time to recover and return energy to the roots for next year's growth. Rhubarb freezes very well. Wash the stems, cut into pieces approximately 3-5cm (1-2 inches) long and place on a tray in the freezer. Once frozen, place the rhubarb in a bag and tie a knot or seal the bag. It stores well for about a year.

CAUTION: the leaves of rhubarb are toxic to humans. Do not eat them.

RHUBARB

As a child I disliked rhubarb; I found it too acidic and the texture seemed rather slimy. In later years, I discovered that it doesn't need to be cooked to a pulp; if I have overcooked it by accident, then mixing it with apples improves the overall texture. A small amount of Sweet Cicely (leaf) can be added to the saucepan while cooking. Its gentle aniseed flavour lessens the sharpness of the rhubarb.

Early varieties of rhubarb, like Timperley Early, can be harvested from late February to July, but I usually wait until late March to start harvesting in earnest. Later varieties will still be growing their tasty, brightly coloured stems and are worth waiting for another month or so before harvesting. Fresh rhubarb feels like such a treat and is among the early season crops that I really value in the kitchen.

When my children were young, we moved to a house with a very empty garden, except for a rather sad and tatty lawn and some very mature rhubarb plants. I was so delighted to have this source of food that I became more than a little over-enthusiastic about it. We had stewed rhubarb, there were crumbles and pies and I made sorbet and ice cream. I even added it to stew! It's not something I recommend because it gave the dish a rather peculiar flavour. We also felt the after-effects of suddenly consuming a large volume of rather acidic, roughage-filled food. Nowadays, I keep the old adage of 'everything in moderation' firmly in my mind; I enjoy rhubarb in early spring, but without going overboard on the amount consumed at one sitting.

Towards the end of the harvesting season, late June to July, the stems become quite tough, but they are ideal for making rhubarb wine. I happily fill the freezer with these larger, tougher stems of rhubarb for wine-making throughout the year. Rhubarb makes a very palatable white wine with a refreshing fruity flavour.

Rhubarb can be grown from seed, but I think the easiest way to acquire new plants is through crowns. A crown is a section of root together with a growing bud, tip or eye. You can purchase them or mature plants can be lifted and divided into pieces before replanting. Lifting a rhubarb plant is not for the faint-hearted, the roots can grow large and woody. Once out of the ground, use a spade or saw to divide the roots with a bud per section. Newly planted crowns should be left to grow for the first year without taking a harvest from them, to allow the roots to develop and the plant to grow strong.

REDUCING PESTS

REDUCING PLACES
FOR PESTS TO THRIVE

Another key aspect to keeping a good balance of pests and predators in your garden is to reduce the number of places that pests can thrive unchecked. Slugs and snails in particular will welcome the dark, damp places offered by overgrown grassy areas or pots and trays left lying around.

USING POULTRY

Chickens and ducks are the most commonly used poultry for pest control. Each bring with them some issues for the gardener. Chickens scratch up the soil, eat the very crops you are growing for food and their faeces can be alkaline, so bedding needs to be stored for a year or more before using in the garden.

Ducks can make a lawn a muddy mess in a short space of time, dibbling holes into the ground, eating your crops and stomping on plants too. However, both are excellent at foraging for insects and ducks make superb slug and snail detectives. If you can allow a pair of ducks (or more) to patrol, they will make a significant dent in the one-footed creature population in your garden.

FLOWERS TO ATTRACT
POLLINATORS AND PREDATORS

Planting flowers among the vegetables can attract pollinators and pest predators. Simple form flowers with an open flower structure (like daisies) attract flying insects to the garden because they are easily seen and offer easy access to their nectar. The more complex the flower, the harder an insect will have to work to access the nectar. I usually plant flowers that are also useful in the kitchen such as Calendula, borage, nasturtium. Herbs also produce flowers that attract insects, like rosemary, chives, dill and fennel.

USING VEG IN THE
FLOWER GARDEN

Likewise, planting vegetables within a flower garden
can bring benefits too. Many vegetables are attractive
plants and there is no reason that they should be hidden away or excluded from the ornamental garden.
I plant herbs, brassicas and salads in the flower beds
to add extra colour, leaf texture and height to the
beds and to act as short-lived ground cover.

ROOT PARSLEY

Also known as Hamburg parsley, this interesting root vegetable is a relative newcomer to our kitchen and garden. Not that it's a new plant, simply that we've only discovered it in the last few years. Sown in spring to early summer, the leaves can be harvested as fresh green parsley, but with the added advantage that the roots can be harvested during the winter and early spring as an alternative to parsnips. They have a parsley taste and texture of parsnips and are pale cream or white in colour. In our garden, they haven't grown large like some of the parsnips do, but as a dual-purpose plant, I feel it is worth sowing a row or two. The roots can be harvested throughout the winter, but by the end of March I have found that they start regrowing and the roots become woody and less appealing. As a member of the umbellifer family, if left they will run to seed providing a show of flat flower heads with hundreds of tiny flowers.

EDIBLE FLOWERS

There are many edible flowers to be harvested during the growing seasons and the early flowers include primrose, dandelion and magnolia.

To eat the flowers, remove the green part behind the petals and the pistils, which are usually located within the centre of the petals. Perhaps it is easier to think of it as 'only eat the petals'.

Borage flowers seem to open at the merest suggestion of sunshine. I grow both blue and white varieties of borage and the blooms of both add a hint of warmer days to our salads. I do not take all the available flowers from a plant because they provide food for any bees or other pollinators that take advantage of the gentle spring sunshine. Winter pansies and violas are also edible; they will flower throughout the winter months and into spring, adding colour to the garden and to the plate. Grown in tubs around the gravel yard of our home in Monmouthshire, they scattered their seeds freely and each year I would carefully lift the young seedlings and transplant them into beds and borders to grow on.

Some flowers are useful as a garnish, but also as a flavouring. Calendula has delicately fragranced petals that can be used as a substitute for saffron. Magnolia petals have a gingery taste and are ideal for making a syrup. The colour of the petals will determine the eventual colour of the syrup.

As with all edible flowers, don't use pesticides or herbicides on or near the flowering plants. I wouldn't eat the flowers from a newly purchased plant because there is no way of knowing what was sprayed on it prior to purchase. Also, the stamens and pistils need to be removed before eating the petals.

Amongst the most abundantly available flowers this month are dandelions. Their bright and cheerful yellow heads are a common sight in fields, verges and in lawns and borders. They attract pollinators and bees and, although not a great source of food for bees because the pollen doesn't contain many of the nutrients they need, they are available at a time when, in many places, few other plants are in flower. For us, dandelion flowers are a good ingredient in syrups, marmalades and wine.

My parents dabbled a little in home-brewing, but not, as far as I recall, in wine making. My father had made pale ale from a kit and he stored the bottles on shelves in the garage. Inevitably, there were a few explosive episodes as the pressure built inside the bottles. I recall, in my early teens, going into the parish meadows and picking dandelion flowers for a good friend's parents to make dandelion wine. I didn't understand their excitement at receiving bucket after bucket filled with yellow petals, all I knew was that my hands were stained for days after picking so many dandelion heads. Nowadays I would be thrilled to be presented with such a haul.

Many moons ago, somewhere in the mid-1990s, I hosted a formal dinner party. I've probably only ever had three or four dinner parties in my life. They are far too much work and too stressful. I'd much rather friends just came for supper and we were informal and all mucked in and the evening was a relaxed affair.

Anyway, I had decided to create something lovely for the dinner party using food from the garden that had been stored in the freezer and fresh ingredients from our local butcher and greengrocer. For dessert I made a champagne jelly. This dish was inspired by something I'd seen on television or read in a book, about Victorian kitchens and dining. It had a light gold clear jelly and suspended within the jelly were primrose flowers gathered from the garden. Talk about fussy cooking! It required me to make the jelly using champagne and leaf gelatine and put some into a fancy jelly mould, then put it into the freezer to help it set quickly, but not set too much. Onto that layer I placed primrose flowers and covered them with more of the liquid jelly. I repeated this process again twice, ending up with three rings of suspended flowers within the jelly. It was a thing of beauty and so fiddly to make that I've never done it since!

HERBS AND SPICES

I could include a section about herbs in every month of the year, but will lump them all together. Herbs are an essential part of my garden and the kitchen. They are what differentiates one meal from another; the same ingredients can be transformed into entirely different dishes by the addition of various herbs and spices.

I grow no plants that might be considered spices. Chillies and peppers are not given room in my growing beds because I am not able to eat them and although I now have a Schezwan pepper tree, it is only knee high and it will be several years before I can gather a small harvest from it. I wish that before I had become intolerant to the capsicum family I had grown some peppers, simply so that I could have had the joy of eating them and knowing that 'I grew that!'

Herbs, on the other hand, are dotted throughout the vegetable garden and food forest; they grow in pots near the kitchen and on the windowsills. During the months when we rely more heavily on stored foods, herbs can transform a potentially dull meal and can transport us to sunnier times by evoking memories through their aromas and flavours.

There are a few staple herbs that I wouldn't want to be without: evergreen sweet bay, rosemary, sage and thyme, short-lived perennials like parsley, sweet cicely, marjoram and the slightly more robust oregano.; herbaceous herbs, such as chives and mint. Making a list of the basic essential herbs proved harder than I imagined and confirms how important these easy to grow plants are in our diet.

Although most can be grown easily from seed, buying pots of growing herbs from a supermarket or garden centre enables us to have fresh herbs instantly and then they can be planted outside once the weather permits. Pots of herbs like basil, parsley and chives can be divided by carefully separating out the plants, ensuring there are roots and top growth in each section. This way you might find you have 20 or more healthy little plants.

What to sow in March

Seeds to sow without heat

- [ ] Beet | beetroot
- [ ] Fava bean | broad bean
- [ ] Brussels sprout
- [ ] Cabbage including red cabbage
- [ ] Carrot
- [ ] Cauliflower
- [ ] Leaf beets
- [ ] Salad leaves
- [ ] Spring onion
- [ ] Radish
- [ ] Kale
- [ ] Leek
- [ ] Mustard leaves
- [ ] Pea | snow pea | mangetout
- [ ] Spinach
- [ ] Turnip

Seeds to sow with heat

- [ ] Celeriac
- [ ] Celery
- [ ] Onion seeds
- [ ] Shallot seeds
- [ ] Tomato (sow eight weeks before last frost date)

APRIL

April feels like a hopeful month. Daffodils, tulips and other spring bulbs burst open offering splashes of colour across the garden. Blossoms on trees open and once again the focus of our eyes moves from beneath our feet to above head height. Garden centres fill their display shelves with annual and perennial plants to entice us to plant more in our gardens. Easter weekend is often the busiest weekend of the year for garden centres, as we shift our focus from inside the house to out.

In mid spring the weather fluctuates between windy, wet, stormy days and dry, clear days that are followed by a frosty night. It's a month of activity in the greenhouse, polytunnel or on the kitchen windowsill as I sow annual vegetables and flowers for the season ahead.

I also think of it as a restless, frustrating month, as the weather is not usually kind enough to direct sow into the soil or to plant out many seedlings in the open ground. If you grow under cover, there is a daily ritual of checking temperatures and deciding whether you need to open and close doors and windows to keep the temperatures from becoming so high that they cook the young plants, or so low that they get frost burn. During April and May, I feel gardening becomes an art form of delicately balanced judgement and action.

TOAD IN THE HOLE

Although there is plenty to sow this month, it is also a good time to finish projects like making raised beds or mending fences. But it is worth remembering that the local wildlife is in full-on spring mode and will be active in your garden, though much of it will be hidden from sight.

Native birds are nesting in trees and migrating birds start arriving from the south to spend their summer in the cooler climate offered by these islands. Spawn in ponds turn into tadpoles and everywhere around us, a new life cycle is taking shape.

When we decided to create a bed for brassicas and put a netting cover over it, we collected some metal pipes to bang into the ground to hold the plastic tubing that would support the netting. The pipes were recycled from a trampoline's legs and had been lying on the ground for much of the winter and early spring. As we banged one of the pipes into the ground, Mr J called me to stop because he had spotted a toad in the pipe. I had already given the pipe one hefty blow with a lump hammer, so its poor little ears must have been ringing. Mr J carefully carried the pipe to a hedge next to the stream that borders our field and the rather surprised animal crawled off to recover from its ordeal.

WINDOWSILL HARVESTS

I've often wondered how long it took for those that came before us to understand which plants could be eaten safely and, in particular, when only one part of a plant is safe to eat, like rhubarb. I'm very grateful that the trial-and-error work has already been done and we can safely enjoy a wide range of tastes in our kitchen without having to worry if this will be the plant that will finish us off. Even so, whenever I try a new fruit or vegetable, I make sure I sample just a small amount to start with. This gives my body a chance to experience the plant with a lower risk of some kind of adverse reaction, I hope!

This month sees a great many seeds being sown and seedlings pricked out or potted on. When I've sown too many of a particular plant, the surplus can be grown on a little, in their seed trays, to use in the kitchen within a month. Many of the seedlings have edible leaves, but not all, therefore it's worth double checking that you are harvesting an edible leaf. For example, I've read that you can eat cucumber leaves when they are small, but they don't appeal to me, or tomato leaves in small amounts, although I've also read that they are toxic.

Like anything in life, do your due diligence, double check your findings with a source you consider reliable before you eat a plant you are unsure about.

Taking time to stop, observe and absorb the changes in our garden, can give us a better understanding of how we interact with and, at the same time, are a part of our environment.

Another way to add to the fresh food in the kitchen is to grow microgreens and sprouted seeds. They are easy to grow all year round and especially useful during the hungry gap. It is only recently that I've realised I've eaten microgreens since I was a small child, we just didn't give them that name. I'm not sure I would have been very impressed at being offered an egg and microgreen sandwich. A simple way to grow microgreens is on some damp tissue in a container on the kitchen windowsill, but equally easy is to fill an additional seed tray with compost and sow seeds thickly over the surface. Stand the seed tray in a container of water to allow the compost to absorb the water from below and then transfer the seed tray into a container that will prevent water dribbling over your windowsill. This latter step matters less if you are growing microgreens in your greenhouse or polytunnel. With a little warmth, it doesn't usually take very long for the seeds to germinate and then a few days to a week or so to provide you with microgreens to cut and add to meals.

Sprouted seeds can be ready in even less time. Seeds are put into a jar and water is added. Surplus water is then drained out and a lid with tiny holes or cloth covering is put on the jar. Seeds should be rinsed in fresh water daily. Once the seeds have started germinating and tiny shoots can be seen, the seeds are ready to eat.

Image courtesy of Kathryn Davies

Hedge of Taunton Deane kale at Incredible Vegetables, Devon

PERENNIAL BRASSICAS

One of the joys of growing perennial kales, cabbages and broccoli is their ability to provide copious amounts of food all year round. Some of the perennial brassicas are so generous and prolific in their growth, that they can even be grown as a hedge!

If you are a lover of the brassica family, they are a useful addition to the kitchen garden, but as they can grow large, it might be worth growing them on the edges of the garden rather than in a raised bed. I grew Taunton Deane kale in a raised bed and it shaded such a large area that little else could grow there. Having learnt my lesson, I carefully chose where to site the kales in our new garden. Taunton Deane is planted in the food forest, where it can grow to a magnificent size without hindering smaller vegetables. Likewise, Daubenton kale is in the food forest, but I have planted the variegated version in a raised bed in the vegetable garden. I plan to use it to take cuttings and will keep it confined to a suitable size through judicious cutting back on a regular basis. Any rooted cuttings of the rather pretty, cream-edged plant will end up in the cut flower field to use as filler material in bouquets.

BEETROOT

I cannot sing the praises of the humble beetroot enough. The purple slices of eye-wateringly vinegary vegetable of my childhood memories have been replaced by sweet, earthy flavours in a variety of colours that please the eye as much as the palette.

Beetroot is traditionally a summer harvest, a few years ago I started sowing beetroot seeds in early autumn. They will sit in the ground throughout the winter and provide an early harvest of small beets in spring. Before the small beetroot are ready to harvest, the new growth of leaves can be used as a hot vegetable. Wilted in a pan with butter, ground black pepper and a light touch of garlic, they are delicious.

Beet seeds sown under cover in late winter and early spring can provide baby leaves for salads. I sow beetroot at regular intervals throughout the year from March to October (and even in November in a mild autumn). For a leaf crop, I sow direct into a raised bed or the ground. For beetroots, I multi-sow in modules early in the year and then direct multi-sow once the soil has warmed sufficiently for the seeds to germinate readily. Multi-sowing is easy, it simply requires you to sow two or more seeds into an area together. For beetroot, I usually sow three or four seeds together.

I used to associate beetroot with the summer months, salads and pickles, but a few years ago I discovered the joy of slow cooked beetroot, either roasted with a variety of vegetables or slow fried over a low temperature, which gives the beet the texture of a good steak. Well not exactly, but not a bad second option.

WATER SUPPLY

Water is an essential component of the garden. Without it, nothing will grow, so it is worth considering how you will ensure water is available to the plants, the soil and even the compost heap. It is even more important to plan how you will supply water to enclosed spaces like a greenhouse or polytunnel.

As our climate continues to change and weather patterns become more extreme, having access to water becomes increasingly urgent during hot, dry summers. Capturing rainwater is the best way to ensure you have some water at the time when your plants need it most. Rainwater is generally kinder to plants than tap water because it has not been processed and had cleaning agents added. It is worth noting that in some areas, particularly in some parts of USA, rainwater collection is not permitted: check in your area before you collect your own. In the UK you can collect rainwater for use in your garden.

It is easy to collect rain by putting buckets out in the open or by collecting it from guttering downpipes. Containers of almost any size can be used and if possible, use a container that light cannot penetrate as this will reduce the chances of algae forming in the water. If the container does not have a lid, create a netting cover to ensure that animals do not fall into the water. Site the water container at the top of a slope so that a gravity-fed hose pipe can be used to water the garden. If your garden is flat or you are unable to collect rainwater at the top of a slope, consider how you will move the water from the container to the soil. Many water butts and containers have a tap on the side of them to allow you to fill a watering can. Or ensure that you have access at the top of the container to scoop water out of it.

If you cannot collect rainwater, using a garden hose attached to a mains water system may be your

only option. There are things that you can do to minimise the amount of water you use in the garden.

- ▸ Do not water in the heat of the day. Early morning or evening watering will allow the water to soak into the ground with less chance of evaporation.

- ▸ Water the soil, not the plants. This is usually better for the plants too.

- ▸ Use a soaker hose system. These have either watering points at regular intervals along a narrow pipe or a leaky hose that slowly releases water along the entire length. Both systems deliver water to the soil and not over the plant, using less water.

CHECKING ON BEES

Although we have had bee hives on our homestead for five years, I am still not entirely comfortable tending to them – actually, quite the opposite – but I want to be. I want to be able to tend the hives to ensure we have healthy, happy colonies of bees. However, until I reach that stage, we have 'Andy the Bees' to care for our apiary.

And so it was, over a warm Easter weekend, that Andy visited our home to inspect the bees for the first time since the autumn. I busied myself with other tasks and then wandered up the hill to see how he was getting on. 'They're a bit feisty today', he said. 'They weren't very happy at having the lid taken off.'

And with that, one of the bees expressed its dissatisfaction with life by flying at me. I'm sure if I could have seen its little bee face, it would have been scowling, but the first thing I knew of it was when I heard the buzzing very close to my ear. The buzzing got louder and I shouted to Andy to come and help get the bee off me. And there was my big mistake! Andy walked quickly towards me, bringing with him several pretty grumpy bees flying around the helmet of his bee suit. They quickly abandoned Andy to help rescue the bee stuck in my hair. So, then I had one in my hair and several bees circling me and bumping me (a warning sign). 'Stand still' Andy calmly said. 'I can't' was my reply as I ran off down the hill, raking my fingers through my hair and flapping my arms around like a windmill in a hurricane.

To say I was scared was an understatement. My hesitancy with beekeeping has stemmed from having a bee stuck in my hair many years ago – it was loud, unpleasant and I found it very frightening. I'm sure the bee was frightened too, but I was left mildly traumatised by the incident. Anyway, I ran down the hill and headed for the wildlife pond, the bees still circling me. On reaching the pond,

I dropped to my knees and without hesitation, dunked my head into the cold, slightly slimy pond water. It took several dunkings on each side to extract the bee that was trapped in my hair and with the loud buzzing gone, I could do a super-fast assessment of the situation. I had been stung on the finger. There was a bee inside my long sleeve t-shirt, so that came off pretty quickly. I brushed a bee out of my bra and shook my t-shirt to try to remove any other bees before putting it back on. I didn't notice that I had been stung twice more under my bra-strap, I guess a bee had got stuck there and panicked.

Shaking, I phoned Mr J at the house and just shouted 'antihistamines!' – I didn't need to say more, he knew that I was in trouble of some kind. By the time he had grabbed the tablets and got outside I was on the way back to the house, in the throes of a minor panic attack, hair soaking wet (and probably slightly smelly) and talking gibberish at him.

In the security of the house, I removed my t-shirt again, a dead bee fell onto the floor and another in the washing up bowl. I headed upstairs to wash my hair in case there were any other little bees stuck in it.

Meanwhile Andy, seeing that I was running away flapping like an albatross trying to take off, headed back to the hives to close the open one, gather his things and come to help. He later told us that he had seen me run to the pond and drop to my knees and enter it head first. He had visions that he would come down the hill to find just my feet sticking out of the pond as I tried to escape the bees!

Lesson learnt from this incident. Don't go near the bees when Andy is tending to the hives unless I am wearing my protective beekeeping suit. I haven't been stung by a bee before, so had no idea how my body might react to it and the good news is that I am not allergic to bee stings. What a relief!

CHARD

I would grow rainbow chard in the garden even if we didn't eat it. The bright stems provide a splash of colour even on the dullest of days. The leaves have a soft sheen which contrasts with the stems. There are white, yellow, red, pink and orange versions with green leaves and also a deepest burgundy red stem with dark green and deep burgundy leaves. Chard is hardy, dramatic and a useful plant in the vegetable garden.

Unlike spinach, chard can be harvested even after it starts going to seed. The remarkable twisted stems appear in the second year as the plant races to produce flowers and seeds. As long as there is space for them in the garden, I leave them to grow into huge striking plants because they provide much sought after fresh green leaves at this time of year. I find large chard leaves unpalatable; they taste too strong, too iron-y. The young leaves, however, are delicious in a salad, omelette or stir fry. I happily remove the medium to large leaves, chop the stems into segments and roast them with lots of garlic in a tray of mixed vegetables. Cooked this way, they taste earthy, but as a contrast to the other vegetables, they make a nice change.

The seeds can be collected or the plant can be left to scatter its seeds. Alternatively, the plants can be added to the compost bin, and once the compost is used on your growing beds, you may find chard seedlings popping up all over the garden. I like this haphazard growth pattern, the young seedlings appearing here and there. But if you prefer your vegetables to grow in neat and tidy rows, remove the chard plant before it sets seed.

Image courtesy of Saronne at Sow, Grow and Cook

What to sow in April

Seeds to sow without heat

- Carrot
- Spring onion
- Beet – leaves and beetroot
- Turnip
- Parsnip
- Hamburg parsley
- Celeriac
- Early and maincrop potato
- Purple sprouting broccoli
- Cabbage
- Kale
- Brussels sprout
- Calabrese
- Broad bean
- Pea | snow pea | mangetout
- Salad leaves
- Red Russian kale for salads
- Spinach
- Arugula or rocket
- Tomato
- French bean for indoor growing

MAY

If April was a restless month, all too often May is filled with impatience. There is still the potential for frost, but as the days lengthen and the air warms, invariably I want to be in the garden rather than inside. I also want to plant tender annuals into the soil, but for the most part, it is more prudent to wait. I'm not known for either my prudence or my patience!

The higher number of daylight hours increasingly invites us outside. The sound of nature becomes louder with an almost constant background noise of birds calling to each other. In 2022, for the first time in my life, I was conscious of hearing a cuckoo. I've heard them on nature programmes on television, but never in real life and it was enchanting. I still felt excited to hear it after a couple of months of cuckooing and all I can say is that I admire their constancy and persistence.

ASPARAGUS

This is one of the most special foods in our harvesting calendar. The harvesting period for asparagus is just a few weeks and I have never grown it in sufficient volume to be bored of eating it by the time the harvesting finishes. This is a perennial vegetable that can be grown from seed, but is more often purchased as one-year- or two-year-old crowns. They are long lived plants and once established, will provide a harvest for twenty years or more.

I haven't found a successful way to preserve asparagus leaving it with an enjoyable texture. Freezing leaves it mushy upon defrosting and canning makes it much too soft for our liking. For this reason, it is one of the few vegetables that we enjoy solely during its harvesting season. Some years we begin harvesting during April and with other weather conditions, it is May, but whenever it is, the spears are appreciated. As a word of caution, asparagus contains asparagusic acid and during digestion it is broken down into byproducts that contain sulphur. This can make your urine smell unusual; there is nothing wrong with your asparagus, it is a natural process of digestion.

When the harvesting period is finished, the fronds of the asparagus grow tall; they are light and almost fluffy in their appearance. They do not block out all the light to the soil below and so that space can be used for another crop. However, planting any root crop is not advisable as the asparagus roots will be disturbed when you harvest the root crop. Strawberries make good companion plants for asparagus. They act as a living mulch, covering the surface of the soil, thus reducing water evaporation and erosion by wind or rain. They don't grow very tall, so still allow air to flow around the asparagus stems. Strawberry plants are fairly shallow rooted, so can be carefully lifted out of the bed when they become less productive.

When you buy asparagus crowns, take care in the preparation of the growing bed and in planting them. Do not harvest from them in the first year after planting and then only lightly in the second year.

Whether you dig a trench or grow them in a raised bed, they will benefit from having well-rotted compost, like animal manure, beneath them, and the crowns should be placed on a mound of soil to support the fragile growing centre, while the roots are spread out across the mound. The roots can then be covered in compost and the tip of the growing point left uncovered.

PEAS, SNOW PEAS, SUGAR SNAP AND MANGETOUT

It is possible to grow peas throughout the winter with a little protection or under the cover of a greenhouse or polytunnel. For overwintering peas, choose a hardy variety. There are two types of peas: smooth skinned peas referred to as round peas (which will grow from a November sowing) and wrinkled peas, which just hold too much water around them and easily rot before they have a chance to germinate. My preferred variety of hardy, round pea is 'Meteor'. It is low growing, therefore needs little support and is less likely to be damaged by winds.

In the past I've sown them in a length of gutter suspended from the frame of the greenhouse and more recently, the frame of the polytunnel. And that works well for harvesting pea shoots to garnish meals or add a little pea flavour to salads. Calling it a little pea flavour does those delicate shoots an injustice; the intensity and full, fresh pea taste that those little stems offer is quite remarkable. But growing them in a length of gutter requires regular attention to watering because the compost can dry out quickly, stunting the growth of the pea plants.

I've also sown directly into the ground. Those that haven't ended up as a tasty snack for mice and other small creatures have grown enough in the late autumn to survive the winter. Equally I have sown them in late February or early March and they have slowly grown away to produce not only pea shoots, but pods during the hungry gap.

Peas sown during April and May, for garden growing outside, are usually of taller varieties. They need some support and will scramble up pea sticks or netting. I'm not enough of a pea connoisseur to have favourite varieties. On the whole, very few peas make it to the kitchen for meals, instead they are eaten as I wander around the garden each day, sampling vegetables as I go.

Mangetout, sugar snap or snow peas will grow happily under cover too, usually taking around 8-10 weeks to produce their flat, sweet pods which are harvested while the peas inside are still immature and tiny dots held within the tasty vegetable wrapper.

If sown in succession, a few seeds every two weeks, a harvest can be obtained throughout much of the hungry gap. I have never been this organised. I sow once and pick a few shoots for use in the kitchen and then leave the plants to grow until the pods are around 7-8cm (3 inches) long, at which point I harvest almost daily. I use some fresh in meals and am then reminded that although we like them occasionally, mangetout (which means 'eat all') is not a priority food for us, so I freeze most of the harvest and consign it to a lonely existence somewhere near the bottom of the chest freezer. I use a few, now and then, in stir-fry meals, but frozen mangetouts tend to lose their firm texture and are rather a let-down. I have thought of using them to make a pea soup, but neither Mr J or I are terribly keen on that either. The lesson that I ought to learn from this annual ritual, is to grow fewer mangetout and limit the number of seeds sown to give us a few tasty meals each year rather than a wasted glut. If there are mangetouts left in the freezer from the previous year, I add them to the compost heap, but of course, it would be better not to sow so many in the first place.

DISPOSAL OF WEEDS

I think it's worth spending a bit of time removing as many roots of perennial weeds as possible. Work on a small area at a time and if you are able, keep your back to the area still to be cleared – it's much more positive to see how much you've already achieved than be faced with a task that's still to be done. I can quite happily stand in a field of weeds and celebrate the small square of weed-free space in front of me. Once you've removed as many roots as possible, cover the area with a mulch to minimise growth of new weeds until you are ready to plant in that area.

Weeds like couch grass (twitch or Bermuda grass), bindweed, stinging nettles, mare's tail and brambles have the amazing ability to continue to grow under cover. They send out roots and runners long distances from the plant centre and appear with vigour elsewhere. It may be a task that you will need to continue to do over the years to come, but it is one that, in my opinion, is worth keeping on top of. A quiet walk around your garden or growing space, collecting a few weeds here and there is time well used. I find a nice way to start the day is with a cup of tea, my own thoughts and a couple of handfuls of weed roots removed.

Disposing of those weed roots is worth getting right. I've learnt the hard way that throwing them onto the ground in a heap is unlikely to halt their growth completely. Many of these plants have the capacity to continue growing, to re-establish their roots or to put out seeds after you've lifted them, spreading them even further across the garden. You could burn them, but lighting fires in the garden isn't a great idea; damp garden materials can create a large amount of smoke and in dry conditions there's a risk of a fire spreading out of control. A very effective method of disposing of pernicious weeds and their roots is to make a liquid fertiliser from them. Keep a lidded container, part-filled with water in the garden and add the roots of unwanted plants into it. Over time they will break down and create a nutrient-rich, rather smelly liquid, which is ideal for using, diluted, to return nutrients to the soil.

As a word of caution, keeping a lid on containers of water in the garden is a sensible idea. In Monmouthshire we had a large plastic barrel without a lid, but it was covered with a wire mesh that I had placed on the top and then pushed the mesh down around the sides of the barrel. One day when I had taken the mesh off the barrel to access the water, Monty (our cat) was 'helping' me in the garden and he lost his footing on the fence and slipped into the barrel of deep water. I am so pleased that I heard the commotion and was able to scoop him out quickly. I dread to think what might have happened if I hadn't been close by at the time. Suffice to say, I became almost fanatical about putting the wire mesh covering back in place each and every time I got water from the barrel. In our new garden, I use a wire panel fixed to the fence and weighed down with a brick as well as chicken wire bent across and down the sides of a barrel, to ensure that animals cannot fall into the water butt.

NO MOW MAY

In 2019, a charitable organisation called Plantlife launched their campaign of No Mow May. The idea behind it is to allow our lawns to grow a little longer and to not cut them during the month of May to give wildflowers adequate time to grow, flower and set seed. This provides much needed foraging plants for bees and other insects at a time when there are generally fewer open flowers.

I had seen friends take part in this campaign and decided that for 2022, we would apply the principles of No Mow May to most of the grassy areas on our homestead. This was easy to do because we still hadn't bought a ride-on mower or compact tractor for our site. I asked Dave to keep pathways cut short, but to allow the rest of the grasses and wild-flowers to grow. And grow they did! An abundance of dandelions, then buttercups and plantains, threaded their way through subtle hues of creams and pinks of the grass seed heads. It was beautiful, uplifting and felt completely right for our land.

May became June and the buttercup flowers turned to seed heads, and hawksbit flowers appeared. The purple flowers of self-heal pushed their way through the shorter grasses, as did daisies and clovers. By July and into August, thistles were blooming, attracting butterflies with their bright purple flowers held above viciously spiky stems and leaves. Spending plenty of time in the garden, observing, feeling a part of all the life around me, I came to appreciate how fuzzy the body of a

It is a good idea to keep some areas mown, but not very short and less frequently. This not only allows for human access, but also a wider variety of wildflowers to grow. Those that are adapted to a shorter sward, simply don't do well among thigh high grasses.

butterfly is or that its antennae are stripy. Things I would have missed if I had been racing from one activity to the next.

As with so many projects, I am good at putting them into practice, however, I am not always so good at thinking through the exit strategy. In this case, how I was going to deal with over two acres of long grass that would need to be cut at some point. In my imagination, we would have acquired a compact tractor with mowing deck by then, but as we hadn't got that organised in the previous twelve months, it was pretty unrealistic of me to think it would suddenly happen in the next month or two.

I am a little fearful about purchasing a piece of machinery to help us manage this land; it's a big purchase and, much like buying a car, I have no idea what key features I need to look for. And so, rather than buying the wrong thing, I buy nothing.

By mid-July, the grass was thigh high and the seed heads had turned into paler shades and sprinkled their seeds to the wind. At two-week intervals, Dave continued to mow the pathways in the food forest and orchard (where the ducks roamed each day). Meanwhile, Mr J was using a strimmer to cut the long grass down.

This labour-intensive method of land management is slow, but it's also incredibly valuable. It has allowed me to observe the patterns of growth, the wildflowers and animals that inhabit the space. In combination with the newly planted trees, shrubs and herbaceous perennials in the food forest, I have seen how wildlife is interacting with the grasses. The overall number of birds at Byther Farm has increased as they come to feed on the grass seeds. Insect numbers have risen too, which should encourage more wildlife to remain here and raise offspring. The long grass and the slow cutting will contribute towards establishing a positive pest/predator balance.

What to sow in May

- ☐ Carrot
- ☐ Kohl rabi
- ☐ Swede | rutabaga
- ☐ Kale
- ☐ Cauliflower
- ☐ Purple sprouting broccoli
- ☐ Chinese kale and cabbage
- ☐ Cabbage – white and red
- ☐ Turnip
- ☐ Parsnip
- ☐ Beet – leaves and beetroot
- ☐ Radish
- ☐ Salsify
- ☐ Root parsley
- ☐ Globe artichoke
- ☐ Cardoon
- ☐ Asparagus
- ☐ Lettuce
- ☐ Spring onion
- ☐ Spinach
- ☐ Sweetcorn
- ☐ Beans – runner and French
- ☐ Pea
- ☐ Pumpkin
- ☐ Cucumber
- ☐ Squash
- ☐ Zucchini | courgette
- ☐ Annual herbs

SUMMER

The warmest months of the year are the ones that I most take for granted. I feel more carefree, frivolous and relaxed. Just like the flowers that turn themselves to face the sun throughout the day, I too spend more time with my head lifted than with my shoulders bent towards the earth.

I have done most of what I can to coax the garden into the shape I'd like it to be for the year and now my role is far more passive. It involves maintenance, observation and long periods of stillness as nature displays its strength and capacity for abundance despite my interference.

For many gardeners, 2022 was a difficult summer for growing food, or more precisely, for keeping plants adequately watered. Much of the UK experienced drought conditions, and while our smallholding saw plenty of rain, there were times when the raised beds needed additional watering and the young trees, planted in the previous few months, suffered setbacks due to dry spells. We also enjoyed (or possibly endured) two heatwaves, recording the highest temperatures on record. Friends and family sent me photographs of grass so dried out that it looked like sand, and trees lost leaves early in response to the stress caused by a lack of water and continued high temperatures. Meanwhile, on our mountainside, the grass was lush and green. This was due in part to adequate rainfall, but also because we had not cut the grass short and I feel that the longer grass cast more shade and reduced the impact of the sun and drying winds on the soil.

JUNE

The first of the summer months is an exciting time with much activity in the garden. The soil has warmed enough for young and tender plants that have been nurtured under the cover of a greenhouse, polytunnel or kitchen windowsill to be planted out.

I take my time in putting each plant into the soil and get into a rhythm of movement.

The flowers planted in beds, borders and the food forest begin to share their colourful blooms, inviting insects to pollinate and for us to admire their wide variety of colours, forms and scents. Leaves on the trees have grown enough to cast dappled shade on the ground below and birds are busy nesting, raising chicks and finding food all around us.

In opposition to planting, I try to keep on top of weeding in the growing beds in this early part of summer. Small plants removed now will not flower and scatter their seeds everywhere. However dull weeding might be as an activity, time spent earlier in the year pays off because it reduces the amount of panicked 'quick before the seed pods open' weeding I need to do later in the year. There is another advantage to carrying out these gentle rhythmic tasks: my thoughts can wander because it doesn't take much brain-power to make a suitably sized hole for a small ball of roots to be planted into or to pull out a self-sown seedling that is in the wrong place. And I can enjoy the warmth of the early summer sun on my back and revel in the experience of being surrounded by and being a part of this abundant natural world.

EXTREMES OF WEATHER

In 2022, nature hadn't quite finished with wintery weather and there were frosts on several nights during the second week of June. Many plants can cope with a little frost, but more tender plants like courgettes and other cucurbits can be damaged, knocked back and even killed by frost. I noticed what I thought was a light frost on the morning of 12th June and discussed it with Saronne (*Sow, Grow and Cook*) when I visited her smallholding that day. On the 14th, she sent me a photo showing the damage done to her plants that morning. It seems that regardless of how much we learn about gardening, no matter how experienced we are as growers, we still need to be vigilant, watch the weather reports and be ready to cover our tender plants when a cold night is predicted.

As our climate changes and weather patterns become different, with more extremes, we will need to adapt our growing practices and potentially be prepared to change what, when and how we grow. As small-scale food producers in our gardens and allotments, we are probably more able to respond quickly to the changes than farmers growing hundreds of acres of monoculture crops. We have the advantages of being able to try small amounts of several varieties to see how well they grow in our microclimate, we can move plants around in the growing space to offer more shelter, more sunshine, and we can watch and respond quickly if there is an issue in the garden. Being so responsive becomes much harder, or maybe impossible, if you have tens or hundreds of acres of plants.

Image courtesy of Saronne at Sow, Grow and Cook

FAVA BEANS

Of the several different types of fava beans, I grow broad beans. As a child I disliked them intensely; I would push them around on my plate hoping that nobody would notice that I wasn't eating them. They had tough little jackets that were an unpleasant texture to chew. There was nothing about them that I liked. Not one bit, not at all!

Given how much I disliked them, I'm slightly surprised that I ever started to grow them as an adult. But Mr J said that he liked them and in a true 'love conquers all' moment, I planted some seeds. The first taste of homegrown, freshly picked broad beans was an eye-opener. I liked them – not just a bit, I liked them all!

Fava beans are among the first of the crops to be ready from an autumn sowing. I like the excitement and the suspense of not knowing how well the beans have formed in the pods and find a gentle but deep joy in opening the pods to reveal the hidden beans.

After a couple of hours of podding the beans, I don't feel quite so much excitement or wonderment, but for a short while each year, I am enchanted.

One could harvest just a few pods at a time, taking just enough for one meal, but I want to use the space that the beans occupy for the

> To save your own bean seeds, place the beans onto some greaseproof paper or a plate, spread them out so that they do not touch each other and leave them on an airy surface, out of direct sunlight, to dry naturally. Once completely dry, store in a paper bag or envelope. Don't forget to label the contents and the date that you collected the seeds.

next crop, so I harvest all the fava beans at once. I store them in the freezer, ready to add to meals whenever we want them. Many people choose to remove the skin of the beans too, but I prefer to leave it on as they contain so much flavour, and life is busy enough without double podding beans.

There is a second crop obtainable from broad beans. The tops of the plants can be pinched out and eaten. They taste of broad beans and are delicious when wilted in a pan with a little butter and splash of water. The tops of fava beans are often pinched out to reduce the risk of aphid attack, although usually the blackfly that are attracted to the tasty young growth do not reduce the harvest of beans by any significant amount. If I haven't already pinched out the tops, I do so when harvesting the pods, increasing the harvest taken to the kitchen.

I usually select a few of the largest, healthiest beans to dry to use as next year's seeds.

INAPPROPRIATE LABELLING

One of the first batches of seeds I sow in early spring are brassicas. In our new home I was eager to get these started so that the perennial cabbages would have a chance to grow to a good size in their first year. I planted them into a newly made raised bed that had been filled with manure, some top soil and bought-in compost and away they grew. I was surprised at the deep green colour of their leaves because the variety of perennial cabbage I prefer has pale, lime green leaves (Paul and Becky's Asturian tree cabbage from Real Seeds). I put the depth of colour down to the richness of the growing medium, after all, the quality of the soil in our Monmouthshire garden had not been terribly good and didn't have 30% composted horse manure in it. Imagine my surprise, while showing a friend around the new vegetable garden, when I spotted heads of calabrese neatly nestled in the centre of each plant!

I have no idea how I mislabelled the seed trays, but I should have paid attention to my initial reaction to the growth of the dark green leaves. Seeds of the much-loved tree cabbage were sown the next day and while we waited for those to grow, we enjoyed the unexpected early summer harvest of calabrese.

As the growing year progresses, I tend to be more lax about labelling plants and in particular seeds that I've sown directly into the soil. I usually mark the start and end of each row with a stick or twig, assuring myself that I'll remember what I've sown. Invariably, I forget and spend a few weeks wondering exactly what it is that is growing in straight neat rows in the vegetable garden!

When we had the roof replaced on our house, the builders kindly reused as many slates as they could, but those that were damaged and couldn't be returned to the roof were thrown in a skip. The recycler in me knew that there would be a better use for some of those broken slates and I spent a merry hour or so rescuing many usable slates from the skip before it was collected. I bought a chalk pen and have created large labels for use in the garden. I think they are more attractive than having small white plastic labels dotted around the garden and because of their size, it is easy to see at a quick glance what is planted.

CURRANTS

Blackcurrants, redcurrants and white currants are straightforward to grow and modern compact varieties allow us to grow them in smaller gardens or where space is at a premium. They propagate readily from cuttings of semi-ripe stems, either in a jam-jar of water on a windowsill or in a pot of compost. I think they are easier to propagate and care for than they are to harvest from!

There are also several crosses of currants, such as josterberry (gooseberry x blackcurrant) or chuckleberry (redcurrant x jostaberry). I grow both of these and enjoy the complexity of taste each provides. As with most soft fruit, I freeze it as soon as it is harvested in small containers, like used, washed yoghurt pots. There is so much to harvest, prune, weed and enjoy at this time of year, I don't really want to waste hours in front of the cooker making jams, jellies, syrups, compotes and wine. Freezing the soft fruits allows me to come back to them at a later time, when the weather is less appealing and warming the kitchen with the heat of the cooker makes the house feel cosy.

Since the 1980s, when cheesecakes became a popular choice on restaurant menus, I have loved blackcurrant cheesecake. The contrasting textures and the slight saltiness of both the biscuit base and the cream cheese juxtaposes with the sweetness of the sugary sauce that coats the acidity of the fruit. I don't know who invented the combination, but I am forever grateful to them for putting it together in one dish. Nowadays I rarely eat in a restaurant. The food we have at home is usually fresher and tastier than anything we can afford to buy cooked by someone else. Added to which, I eat a gluten free diet, so home-grown and homecooked food allows me to carefully monitor exactly what I'm eating. To replace those wonderfully creamy, stodgy slabs of cheesecake of my memory, I make a deconstructed cheesecake alternative. It's easily made by placing gluten-free rolled oats in a bowl, spooning some quark or other soft cheese over them and adding some fresh or frozen blackcurrants on top. A spoonful of honey or agave syrup adds sweetness. And although it doesn't quite meet the mark for a stodgy slab, it comes pretty close.

The majority of the currant bushes are growing in the food forest. Apart from the currant hedge, the plants are spread out across the half acre area. My thinking behind this is that should a pest find one plant, it is less likely to pass from plant to plant if there are large spaces between them.

Encouraging predators into the garden is by far the most effective way to deal with aphids and other pests in the long run. Inevitably, the aphids will arrive and build a population before the predators arrive, but as the garden matures, the pest/predator balance will improve and aphid attacks will become less obvious.

Each year some of the bushes show signs of aphid attack. The aphids live on the underside of the leaves, sucking the sap from the leaves causing the leaves to distort and come up in red blisters. It is unsightly, but the aphids do not usually affect the vigour of the plant or the production and quality of the currants. I see no point in trying to remove them by hand, especially when I have plenty more pressing things to attend to. They are a food source for predators such as ladybirds, hoverflies, ground beetles and earwigs.

WEEDS IN THE GROWING BEDS

A plant that I consider a nuisance weed may be precisely what another gardener wants in their garden. For example, whenever I publish a video that shows me pulling dandelions from the pathways of the raised bed vegetable garden at Byther Farm, I receive more than a few comments and messages asking why I'm disposing of a valuable vegetable. The answer is very simple; neither Mr J nor I like the taste of them. I know that dandelion flowers are a great food resource for bees and indeed, in the area close to the beehives, I leave the dandelions to grow and flourish.

There are areas of our smallholding that we leave to nature, where the weeds are welcome to grow, set seeds and spread. But those plants will compete for the same light and nutrients that our food crops require, so a little judicious weeding tips the balance in favour of the food plants and flowers that we are nurturing.

HAND WEEDING

Hand weeding is exactly as it implies; the process of using your hands to remove unwanted plants. It is ideally suited for removing weeds that grow in among the plants that you do want to grow, especially where they are growing close together and using a tool might damage your vegetable, fruit or flowering plants. It can be time-consuming and boring but there are ways to reduce the amount of hand weeding that needs doing. Disturbing the soil as little as possible, mulching, and the density of planting can impact on the numbers of weed seeds that germinate in your growing beds.

USING A HOE

Hoes are specifically designed to sever the stems from the roots of plants either on or just below the soil surface. The key to successful hoeing is to use a very gentle action, running the blade of the hoe backwards and forward just a centimetre or so under the surface. The weed tops and roots can then be left on the surface of the soil to wilt and die. Hoeing is ideal for small annual and perennial weeds that do not have large root systems.

CHOP AND DROP

'Chop and drop' is a great way to deal with weeds if they have grown a little larger, if you are reducing weeds in an area that has either become overgrown or where you've left them to grow for the benefit of wildlife. It involves cutting the green leaves and stems and dropping them onto the ground to form a mulch that decomposes over time. You can also add them to the compost heap, for example, I like to add dock leaves.

If the weeds have seed heads on them, you can either take them off and put them in a container of water to rot down or you can leave them on the plants and drop them on the ground. The risk of leaving them on the plants is that the seeds could then germinate at a later date.

LETTING WEEDS GROW A BIT

A more contentious practice is to leave the weed seedlings to grow a little. I do this regularly for two main reasons. Firstly, I want to be sure that the plants I'm removing are of the unwanted variety. Over time, gardeners become familiar with the seed leaves (those first couple of leaves that break through the seed shell), but many seedlings look very similar. By leaving them to grow a little, I can double check that I'm not about to pull up, hoe or chop and drop a plant that I would like for elsewhere in the garden or even one that could grow exactly where the seeds have landed and started to grow. Secondly, I made a choice about how often and for how long I am prepared to spend weeding the garden in comparison to other tasks or observation and relaxation time. The compromise I make is that each month, some areas of the garden are left for the weeds to grow a little taller before they are removed.

CALABRESE

This easy to grow vegetable is instantly recognisable from its large head of tight green flower buds and is often labelled 'broccoli' in stores and markets. Seeds sown from spring to early summer produce strong plants with large leaves and a single large flower head. Having grown so many of them in error during 2022, I am now convinced that they will be a regular feature in our vegetable garden. Staggered sowings will

To prevent leafy vegetables from wilting in your kitchen, stand the stems in a container of water. Refresh the water at least once a day.

provide a continued supply of calabrese that can either be eaten fresh or frozen for enjoying during the winter months.

As yet I haven't worked out how to freeze calabrese so that it still has an 'al dente' texture once defrosted, but experimenting over the coming years will, I hope, find the answer.

LETTUCE AND SALAD LEAVES

Although lettuce and salad leaves can be grown and harvested year-round, it is usually during June that the first of the spring sown lettuce heads are ready for harvesting. Increasingly I grow lettuce that can be harvested on a cut-and-come-again basis, because a loose-leaf lettuce will continue to produce new leaves, providing us with fresh salads, over a period of weeks. But there is something jolly satisfying about harvesting a whole head of lettuce and taking it to the kitchen to wash and prepare for a meal. These moments of intense satisfaction are worth noting, remembering and celebrating.

In recent years, I have grown a lettuce called Salanova Expertise RZ (79-27). It's not a terribly enticing name, but the lettuces are superb. It was developed for the commercial grower, but is now available for home growers. The seeds I purchased are coated with a thin layer of clay, which makes sowing them individually very simple. The leaves are frizzy and densely packed and the plants are tolerant of heat and less likely to bolt than most lettuces. I've never seen a lettuce with quite so many leaves and although the seeds are not cheap, I think they are good value for the sheer amount of lettuce each plant produces. I also like the texture and taste of this lettuce, so for me it's a good choice.

I also enjoy Romaine lettuces and grow a tricolour selection. The individual plants are either green, red or flecked, but the seed packet offers all three varieties and it makes for a pretty bowl of salad. I've also found that, like all lettuces, if left in the ground it will flower and produce seed. However, unlike most lettuces I've seen which have yellow flowers, Romaine lettuces produce intense blue flowers that are worthy of any flower border.

What to sow in June

- ☐ Beans: Runner and French
- ☐ Carrot
- ☐ Beet | beetroot
- ☐ Leaf beet
- ☐ Calabrese
- ☐ Chinese cabbage
- ☐ Kohl rabi
- ☐ Cucumber
- ☐ Zucchini | courgette and marrow
- ☐ Summer squash
- ☐ Winter squash
- ☐ Pea
- ☐ Radish
- ☐ Rutabaga | swede
- ☐ Purple sprouting broccoli
- ☐ Sweetcorn
- ☐ Summer and New Zealand spinach
- ☐ Turnip
- ☐ Herbs

JULY

July feels like the start of the plentiful season. Flowers are blooming, fruit is developing on trees and bushes and vegetables fill the beds with food. The ground has been warmed. The summer air caresses and strokes our skin and the sunlight brings the promise of balmy evenings.

Colours look clear and bright and my eyes are focussed, neither on the ground, nor up among the leaves of trees, but somewhere between, among the growth of the herbaceous plants and annual vegetables. All around us, wildlife is finding food for its offspring; young birds are fledging, butterflies dance their brief courtships on the wing and caterpillars gorge themselves on nettles, nasturtiums and brassica plants. Inevitably, some years, earlier months are dry and some rainy but, whatever the weather, plants seem to catch up during July and offer abundance for the next few months.

These summer days bring with them an intense happiness; my senses are almost overloaded with stimuli and I'm full of energy. Working with the daylight hours, I tend to be in the garden around 5am, pottering, enjoying the quietness, free from external activities and interruptions and equally, revelling in the hectic comings and goings of life within, and above, the garden.

I return to the house when my stomach reminds me that I haven't eaten since the evening before. Much of my day is spent at the computer or on the telephone, but as the most intense heat of the day starts to subside, I return outdoors. Pottering in the garden in the cooler parts of the day allows me to be more productive and also reduces the risk of sunburn.

One of the unexpected features of our new home is the sheer volume of flying insects that bite, or as Mr J's aunt would have called them 'small bad animals'. It hadn't occurred to me that moving to land previously used for mainly equestrian purposes, that is surrounded by farmland with larger farm animals, might bring with it a marauding horde of small bad animals that see us as nothing more than another walking, all-you-can-eat buffet!

And yet, at the same time I am delighted that there are so many insects and pollinators flitting about from dawn to dusk, with a further fleet of insects doing nocturnal duty.

POTATOES

Is there anything more exciting in the veg growers' year than harvesting the first potatoes? For such a basic vegetable, the spud evokes a great many emotions. The internet has thousands of videos showing potato harvests and it seems our appetite for sharing in another gardener's potato harvest joy or misery is endless. Having made several potato harvest videos, I can confirm that the anticipation and excitement cannot adequately be conveyed through the medium of video.

Planted in spring, the seed potatoes grow away until early to midsummer when they flower, indicating that there may also be tubers forming below the surface. Potatoes are not difficult to coax into growth and you don't need a huge amount of gardening skill to nurture a plant to the point of harvest. Nonetheless, there is something magical about searching in the soil for the hidden treasures that a potato plant offers. It's as though nature designed a lucky-dip game for gardeners!

There are two basic types of potato, determinate and indeterminate. Determinate potatoes produce tubers at the same level as the seed potato, whereas indeterminate potatoes will produce tubers at various levels up the stem. To gain maximum yield from indeterminate potato plants, the stems need to be covered with soil, compost or other growing medium as the plant grows. This process is called hilling or earthing up. Regardless of which type of potato you grow, it is a good idea to hill around potato plants as this excludes light from the growing tubers and prevents them turning green.

One of the greatest joys while learning about no dig gardening was discovering that I could grow potatoes without digging trenches and without having to earth up using heavy soil. I continue to be so delighted at this method of growing potatoes that I share it with anyone who will listen. I grow potatoes on the surface of the compost or soil and cover the seed potatoes with either hay, used duck bedding, grass clippings or a combination of these. To hill up the potato plants I apply more used duck bedding, grass clippings or hay. I do not use straw because in our wet climate, the straw becomes an ideal home for slugs and the potatoes are a tasty meal for them. Hay is usually more dense than straw, making it slightly less welcoming to gastropods.

To harvest no dig potatoes grown under hay or grass clippings (which when dried are the same as finely chopped hay), the mulch can be pushed away from the soil to expose the potato harvest. You can also plunge your hand into the hay or grass clippings and feel around

Green potatoes contain chlorophyll, as do all green plants, but the presence of chlorophyll in potatoes indicates that there is likely to be a high level of glycoalkaloids, substances that our bodies find toxic. Therefore, do not eat green potatoes. However, if you do have green tubers, all is not lost as they can be kept and used as seed potatoes the next year.

for a few potatoes. This allows you to harvest what you need for one meal and leave the remainder to continue growing.

In one of my highly unscientific trials, I tested to see whether there was a difference in yield when applying a mulch of used duck bedding compared to a new bale of organic hay. There was a huge difference, not only in the yield, but in the ease of harvesting. The potatoes grown under the used duck bedding fared much better and the soil beneath the tubers became friable rather than remaining heavy. Without a doubt, in future I will either apply used duck bedding or layers of hay mixed with wood chips or wood shavings and a well-rotted manure of some kind.

FRENCH BEANS

On a windy site, dwarf or bush beans are most practical. My preferred varieties include the yellow podded Polka or Sonesta, a purple podded variety called Purple Teepee and a green podded variety, Tendergreen.

French beans tend to be self-fertile and don't cross-pollinate very often. This makes them ideal for growing several varieties in close proximity. I've grown both bush and climbing French beans and each has its virtues. I find bush beans to be more awkward to harvest, they involve bending and stooping or grovelling around on my hands and

> For all the foods we store, finding the balance of what is easy to grow and what you like to eat is essential. To make the most of the space and time available, grow high value foods, which are usually those that need to be picked by hand and quickly deteriorate.

knees, whereas climbing beans require a support system to twine around, but offer the tasty pods at a level that's kinder on the knees and back.

Each year, the first meal that includes French beans is such a treat. It makes me feel that I have achieved, that I've succeeded in providing us with food for another year, or another season at least! They are sweet, firm and slightly squeaky between the teeth and I love them for it. As with any food that we haven't had fresh for a while, they take on a special significance and we savour the moment. We both know that within a month we will be fed up with seeing them on our plates and within a couple of months, the fresh beans will be over and we'll rely on stored beans until the next year.

More often than not I freeze them, without blanching them first, in bags containing enough for one meal for the two of us. In 2016, I filled the freezer with whole French beans and sliced runner beans. It looked very impressive, but it was a waste of resources. We simply don't eat that many green beans in a year, and by 2019 I was still finding bags of sliced runner beans complete with freezer burn lurking in the bottom of the chest freezer. Now I grow fewer plants, freeze fewer beans and have a much wider range of vegetables in the freezer. I have also started pressure canning some foods and French beans are ideal for this. They look ugly in the glass jars, but are quick and easy to add to stews and stir fry meals that don't call for pretty ingredients.

ORGANIC MULCHES

Mulching serves multiple purposes in the garden. It forms a barrier that excludes light from reaching seeds, potentially giving fewer weed seeds a chance to germinate. Mulch reduces the impact of wind on the soil, lessening the chances of wind erosion. It can prevent water evaporation, holding moisture in the soil even on hot days. Mulching can add nutrients to the soil, increase its microbial life and improve the soil structure, all without us doing anything more than placing the mulch on the surface. Insects, invertebrates and microbial life will work on the mulch without any additional input from us.

Almost any layer of material that will rot down can be used as a mulch, although some materials are decidedly better for some tasks than others.

- **Straw**. During the late autumn, I add a layer of straw on top of the soil in any empty raised beds. It does little to improve the nutrient levels, but it will form a mat over the surface excluding the light and reducing weed growth, it protects against wind and water erosion and deters the neighbourhood cats from digging the soil. In the spring, I remove the straw and add it to the compost heap to continue breaking down. Covering each bed and then removing the straw takes just a few minutes and I feel it is worth the effort for the time it saves in weeding, added to which we are also protecting the soil.

- **Grass clippings**. From spring to autumn, I use grass clippings as a mulch. Do not use grass clippings that have been sprayed with weedkillers for at least three weeks after application (preferably don't use these selective weedkillers on your grass). Sprinkled very finely on the surface of the soil, grass clippings will help to feed the soil. Used in a deeper layer of 5-8cm it will reduce water evaporation, warm the soil and as the top layer of grass dries it forms a mat that weed seeds find harder to germinate in or for young seedlings to grow up through. Slightly deeper layers of grass clippings are used to exclude light from around potato plant stems, preventing the tubers from becoming green and encouraging more tubers to be produced on the stems of indeterminate potato varieties (these varieties will grow tubers from the stem rather than only at the level of the seed potato).

A word of warning about using grass clippings as a mulch: if you lay the clippings too thickly or if you compact them, the layer may start to break down anaerobically. This becomes a black, slimy and often very smelly layer. To prevent this, fluff up the grass clippings as they are placed on the soil to ensure plenty of oxygen is in the layer. Another way to avoid this is to mix the grass clippings with some carbon material, like wood shavings, dry leaves or shredded paper.

- **Wood chips**. I like using wood chips as a mulch, but it's worth getting to know the different types of wood and their potential uses in the garden.

- **Homemade and purchased compost**. Compost is an ideal mulch. Whether you buy in compost or make your own, it will protect the soil from wind and rain erosion, inhibit weed growth and improve the soil structure, nutrient levels and, if using homemade compost, add to the microbial life in your soil. There is no need to dig compost into the soil, using a mulch will do more for your soil. Earthworms will come to the surface and take the compost down into lower levels, incorporating it as they do and also creating tunnels that allow air to flow and water to percolate through the soil.

RASPBERRIES

Autumn fruiting raspberries don't just produce fruit in the autumn. They often start ripening in July and continue to produce berries until late October or even into November. The earliest raspberries are eaten straight from the plant, preferably warmed by the sun. The berries explode in the mouth and the aroma of raspberries fills the nasal cavity. But by late September, with cooling temperatures, the raspberries are firmer and these are the ones I prefer to save for winter and spring.

I also make raspberry jam and raspberry wine. We had three raspberry patches in Monmouthshire and I plan on having a similar number of plants in our new gardens. It will take a couple of years or so for the plants to multiply and fill out their allotted spaces and in the meantime, we have plenty of raspberry jam and other fruits in storage to tide us over.

Freeze raspberries on a tray, making sure that they are spread out and not touching each other, and then, once frozen, transfer them into bags. It makes it easy to pour a few into a bowl rather than a large clump that won't come apart.

I don't like to buy raspberries in a store. They are incredibly expensive because harvesting is labour-intensive. They don't taste as nice as homegrown berries and get mouldy very quickly, and if they don't get mouldy, then I'm worried about how they might have been treated to prolong the shelf life. I would rather go without them.

CUCUMBER

The first time I saw a cucumber plant laden with fruits with little prickles on the skin, I was fascinated. I'm less fascinated by their taste, but they are a useful addition to salads and chutneys. Sown in late spring and planted into their final positions after the risk of frost has passed, they scramble up strings or wires or sprawl across the floor. Regular and even watering is needed to prevent the fruits from having a bitter taste, but apart from that, I find cucumbers easy to grow and relatively trouble-free.

The plants can become large, occupying 1.2 metres (4 feet) or more in each direction and more in height, so it is worth giving them plenty of room. Like most cucurbits, they can be heavy feeders and respond

well to rich soil or to being fed during the growing season. That said, I've grown cucumbers in some shockingly poor soil and although they didn't provide a glut of fruits, they were sufficient for some salads.

I usually grow cucumbers under the protection of a greenhouse or polytunnel, but there are varieties that will happily grow outside and I've had some successes. Wherever you grow them, they are likely to be affected by powdery mildew. Unless the mildew covers all of the leaves, it is unlikely to cause an issue with the production of cucumbers. At the first signs of powdery mildew, pick off the affected leaves and dispose of them in the compost heap.

A glut of cucumbers calls for some imaginative recipes. I've made a hamburger relish, added them to chutneys and even used them to make a creamy cold soup. It was surprisingly peppery and made a delicious starter.

GARLIC

I usually plant garlic cloves in late autumn for harvest from the middle of June to July. There are also some spring planting varieties which are ready to harvest from July to autumn.

Nature neatly provides us with a clear sign when garlic is ready to harvest: the leaves turn yellow.

As with onions, shallots, leeks and elephant garlic, garlic should be lifted from below rather than pulled up by the leaves. This technique prevents any damage to the bulb or the leaves being crushed, which can reduce its storage life.

Using a trowel or hand fork, gently prise the bulb out of the ground. Leave the roots intact. Lay the garlic on a flat surface or hang on a rack in a dry, airy place until the leaves and roots have dried. Store by plaiting or in a basket that allows air to flow around and through it.

What to sow in July

- ☐ Carrot
- ☐ Bean
- ☐ Pea
- ☐ Beet | beetroot
- ☐ Turnip
- ☐ Chard
- ☐ Chicory
- ☐ Spring onion
- ☐ Radish
- ☐ Winter spinach
- ☐ Winter salad leaves

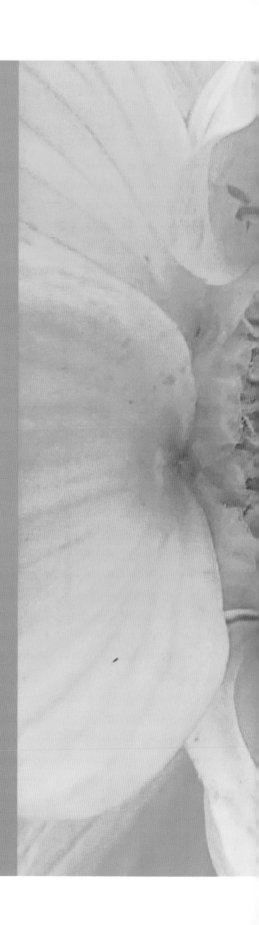

AUGUST

The last month of summer is often a mixture of rainy days that nourish the soil, winds that pull at tall climbing plants and gloriously warm days filled with the sweet scents of flowers. It's a time of plenty, when harvesting becomes a daily ritual of picking beans, berries, cucurbits, roots and leaves. Mornings and evenings have a golden hour, when the sunlight makes the garden look magical. Meals are light and filled with fresh flavours. The vegetable garden looks heavily laden; even the beds where I've harvested and replanted a second or third crop of the year seem to be bursting at the seams, aching under the weight of the abundance. For a vegetable gardener, these are the glory days, the highlights, the moments in our gardening year that we'll look back on and look forward to. And, as much as the day could be filled with harvesting, tending, weeding, clearing and mulching, the activity that I treasure the most is being still. The conscious decision to stop my physical activity and observe and absorb the sights, sounds and smells all around fills me with joy and peace.

SUMMER SQUASHES

Summer squashes including courgettes, known in many places as zucchini, have the uncanny ability to swell from subtle little bite size fruits to marrow size monsters in what seems like the blink of an eye. Sown in late spring and planted out after the risk of frost has passed, the plants positively sprint to grow and produce seeds. The plants can either be bush-like or have a tendency to climb or trail. They have large leaves and slightly spiky stems (and undersides to the leaves) which by August often look tatty and show signs of powdery mildew. The flowers are produced in abundance, first the male flowers borne on straight stems, followed by the female flowers which have a swelling behind the flower. It is this that becomes the fruit. Bees seem to love the deep buttery-yellow flowers which can, if that's your thing, be dipped in batter and fried.

Summer squash fruits come in a variety of colours, shapes and sizes. Colours range from darkest green, which appears almost black, through to palest green, white, yellow and speckled. Shapes and sizes vary too, from the familiar sausage shaped fruits to round or even flying saucer shaped Patty Pan and curled Tromboncino. It is worth noting that many of the yellow fruited varieties may have partly or completely yellow leaves; this is not a sign of lack of nutrients, but is the plants natural colouring.

Most summer squashes are prolific in their fruit production and it is easy to find you have a glut during mid to late summer. The fruits can be sliced, chopped or grated and frozen; they do not need blanching before freezing. I've fallen into the trap of freezing vast quantities of summer squashes and then struggle to find enough storage space for other food. I now only freeze enough for two or three meals, slicing them lengthways to use as an alternative to lasagne sheets. The remainder are eaten fresh, made into chutney or donated to friends and neighbours. Chickens will often eat them, although I remember our chickens looking disinterested in them after three weeks of daily offerings!

The key to not being completely swamped with summer squash is to limit the number of plants grown. It is all too easy to look at twelve or fourteen seeds and think we might as well plant them all, but given the correct conditions for growth, squash tend to have a good germination rate. If, like me, you find it hard to dispose of seedlings, you then end up with far too many plants in the garden, all merrily producing an abundance of fruits. It is better to save the precious resource of seeds for the next year or to sell or donate plants, than to use the limited space in your garden beds for growing food that won't be consumed.

I have seen it suggested that two plants per person in the household is sufficient. I think this is rather generous and, in our garden, one plant per person seems more than adequate. When I had a larger household, I grew one plant for two people. If you find you don't have enough courgette, patty pan or other summer squash for your needs in the kitchen, you are likely to find another gardener nearby who will be delighted to have a new home for their glut of fruits.

Do not remove all the male flowers at once – they are needed to pollinate the female flowers and produce fruits. Continue to pick fruits on a regular basis to encourage the plant to produce more.

After sowing carrot seeds into moist soil, cover with a plank of wood or some netting folded into several layers, to provide a protective covering for the seeds. Check their progress daily and as soon as the tiny green leaves can be seen poking through the soil, remove the cover and give them access to sunlight and water.

CARROTS

We continue to harvest carrots. Sown in succession throughout spring and early summer, carrots are another mainstay of our diet. Some years I have great success with carrots, others are a total wash-out. During our first year in Monmouthshire, I sowed in excess of 3000 carrot seeds, but harvested just six lonely carrots. Fortunately, I now grow hundreds of carrots successfully, providing an abundance for home use and plenty to add to veg boxes or donate to friends, family and our local community food larder.

The difference between the two results is the amount of protection provided for the newly sown carrots. In the first year, I left the seeds covered with a light sprinkling of soil. Heavy rains and strong winds washed the seeds from their place and the protective netting that I had placed around the bed was blown over the ground repeatedly, rubbing away at the surface of the soil and moving the seeds about. Then the sun shone, dried the ground and displaced the carrot seeds that didn't germinate. Once I began to use the advice of James Prigioni, a gardener with an abundant food forest in New Jersey, USA, I had carrot growing success.

I do not sow carrot seeds terribly thinly and I do not thin them out as they grow. I allow them to grow in a thick line of plants and harvest them as young-ish carrots. It's a purely personal preference for the sweetness of the younger carrots. If carrots are grown on to a larger size, for example, more than 2cm (1 inch) thick, I often use them in a mixed root vegetable mash or puree. The combination of carrot and swede (rutabaga) is a firm favourite.

After growing many different varieties of carrot, I have settled on a few that I grow each year, comfortable in the knowledge that we like the flavour and I understand their growth habits.

Carrots offer one further delight which, until a few years ago, I was unaware of. If left in the ground to grow for a second year, carrots produce creamy white flower heads with an intense scent. I had left some carrots to grow with the idea of collecting the seeds and was amazed to find the perfume from the carrot flowers filled the polytunnel with its heady, sweet, almost cloying smell. I remember showing Huw Richards this one (pictured) and we both stood and marvelled at the unexpected beauty and aroma. Nowadays, we both grow carrots not only for their harvest, but for the flowers that attract pollinators and fill us with joy.

Sowings made earliest in the year include Amsterdam varieties and Nantes 2, while summer sowings are usually Autumn King. I also grow some yellow, white and purple varieties, more for the visual interest on the plate than the taste.

CELERY

We have an odd relationship with celery; I find the taste too strong, even overpowering in many dishes, and yet it seems to be an essential ingredient for making really nice stock or for stews because it brings out the flavour of so many other ingredients. A few years ago, I tried a variety called Red Soup, which as its name suggests, was ideal for cooking with. Eaten raw, it was far too intense in flavour for our palate and only a small amount was needed in cooking. I will try again with a different variety in the coming years.

Seeds are sown early in the year on the surface of the compost and the young plants grow steadily indoors or under heated cover until the risk of frost is past. Celery can be blanched as it's growing, a process of excluding light from the stems which makes the stems more tender, milder and sweeter in flavour. Celery does not need to be harvested all at once, it will stand in the garden quite happily until the first frosts of autumn and winter.

As a teenager, I worked in a local restaurant and I was constantly surprised by how many diners chose braised celery as a vegetable side dish. In my head I would shout, 'do you not realise how strong this stuff is?', and I put my dislike of it down to my inexperienced palate. Forty years later, however, my opinion hasn't changed very much; I still find both the texture and taste awkward in the kitchen when eaten on its own. I do use it to add depth to soups and stews, and very occasionally to stir-fry meals, but I use it sparingly. Because of this, I don't give it space in the vegetable garden and use lovage as an alternative in cooking.

EGGPLANT / AUBERGINE

I've always thought aubergines were pretty disgusting; I didn't like the taste, the texture, or even the smell. But about four years ago I decided to grow some, more from curiosity than anything else, and my mind was changed. I planted some seeds of a long, finger-like variety and they were delicious. Since then, I've eaten plenty, in a variety of dishes, and enjoyed them every time.

This pattern of finding I like homegrown vegetables more than store-bought repeats itself time and again. I have finally learnt that it is worth growing vegetables that I have previously not liked, because our taste preferences can change over time and homegrown food, grown from seed selected for taste, can be vastly different to that grown from seed designed for the mass production of easily harvested food.

Seeds of eggplants are sown early in the year and require some warmth to entice them to germinate. Coming from warm climates, they like steady warmth, so growing them under cover is ideal, and regular watering to encourage them to grow into bushy, healthy plants. My plants liked the heat of the summer in 2022, producing numerous fruits.

It is no coincidence that many dishes containing eggplants also feature tomatoes. They ripen at similar times and complement each other's flavours. If you like them, I think it's worth experimenting with different varieties, because not all eggplants look or taste the same. There are purple, white, green and striped-skin varieties and differing shapes too.

For storage, they can be frozen in slices or cubes or pressure canned, but I find freezing them in homemade meals the best way. This is because the preparation and cooking has already been done, the eggplants have absorbed all the flavours of the other ingredients and, as with other ready-made meals, they can be taken from the freezer and defrosted for eating without any further work being needed.

BALANCE OF TIME

Don't forget to factor your time into your garden plans. If you can attend to your garden on a full-time basis, it is easier to plan on a larger or more demanding scale, but be realistic. How much time can you give to your garden? How much time do you want to spend tending your garden? How much purely as leisure time?

It is easy to get carried away with ideas that turn out to be incredibly time-consuming, not just during the setting up phase, but forever more. For example, I love the look of neatly clipped box hedges around flower beds – they add definition and substance to a bed. However, I now know that I am not self-disciplined enough to keep up with the trimming and clipping of such hedges, the result being that instead of neat straight lines, my beds would look overgrown and chaotic; the exact opposite of what I'm aiming for!

I have always regretted following my more elaborate or intricate ideas. And I've almost resented the garden areas that have taken time away from gently enjoying the garden. Or that have stopped me from simply sitting in the garden observing and being a part of the natural story unfolding around me.

It is better to start more simply and expand or change the garden as you get to know your own work patterns, energy levels and wishes for your garden space.

Over the last few years, I've learnt that I can easily manage a vegetable garden that is the size of a full allotment plot (ten rods or poles), which is equivalent to 250 square metres. If I want to tend more space than that, I need to accept that the additional land will not be as neat and tidy or have attention as often as the vegetable garden. The way that I do this is to have areas that are designated as wildlife spaces, an orchard (even if a mini-orchard as in our last home) and food forest. In each of these, my expectation is for it to look messier, wilder and more natural. After fourteen months at our new site, these areas are starting to take shape. I imagine that it will take two or three more years for the newly planted trees and shrubs to settle into their new home and flourish.

MELON

As a child I regularly visited my grandfather, who had retired to the south of Spain. At the local market, the man who sold melons would cut out a square plug of melon for us to sample. What a treat that was! He taught us to smell the end of the melon fruits to assess how ripe they were. Whether the stallholder gave everyone small pieces of melon to try or whether it was just for the curiously blond grandchildren of the old man who lived on the hill, I will never know. But I do recall how special those melon tasters were to me and how grateful I was in later life to have learnt the skill of choosing ripe melons from the store. Squeezing and pushing your finger or thumb into the skin of a melon potentially bruises it and returning it to the shelf then leaves it for someone else to buy bruised fruits. Careful handling and using our olfactory senses seem much better ways to select which melons to buy and which to leave behind.

Melons are another of the cucurbit family of plants. Sensitive to temperature, seeds do not germinate and young plants do not flourish in cold conditions. Seeds sown at the end of April or throughout May grow rapidly. Melons can take up a great deal of space and are ideal for growing up a vertical structure like a trellis or bean netting. I have used twine netting, which looks like a string cargo net, with good results.

The taste of a ripe, homegrown melon is what I imagine ambrosia to be like. Full of juice, sweet and almost cloyingly aromatic; I feel that they are worth the space in the polytunnel or greenhouse, even if you only harvest a small number of fruits from them. That said, I haven't found a way to store melons, so they need to be eaten within a short time of harvesting, which makes them a luxury item. If space is limited and your budget is tight, then growing fruit or vegetables that can be stored in the pantry or freezer might make more sense.

CHILLIES AND PEPPERS

We don't grow any members of the capsicum family, because I have become intolerant to them, but I miss the warming, spicy flavours that they offer to the kitchen menu. Varieties range from mild and sweet to blow-your-socks-off hot and as a general rule, the smaller the fruit, the hotter it is likely to be. Many types of peppers and chillies are worth growing for their ornamental value, with a wide range of colours, shapes and sizes to choose from.

I particularly liked long, sweet peppers that had been roasted in the oven with a merest hint of oil and some garlic cloves. They would caramelise and become even sweeter. Once out of the oven, I'd crumble some feta over them and add a few black olives and eat the dish with a chunk of crusty bread.

Seeds need to be sown very early in the year with some heat to encourage them to germinate. The plants will need steady warmth and light to thrive. Plants need sufficient water to grow and set fruit, but once the fruits are forming, heat from the sun and reduced watering will give a tastier, spicier fruit.

When you have been handling peppers and chillies, avoid touching your face or using the bathroom until you have thoroughly washed your hands.

Image courtesy of ChilliChump

Image courtesy of Anna Murphy

Bell and sweet peppers can be sliced and frozen. Most capsicums can be canned or made into sauces and pastes and preserved by freezing or canning. Chillies can also be dried for storage. As I don't use them, I'm not going to offer further advice other than to say my first stop for more information would be with Shaun and Caroline at ChilliChump.com

HONEY

In late August 2022, when Andy arrived to tend to the beehives, I was happy to show him around the garden, where we admired several different species of bees enjoying the flowers. Their heads buried deep into each flower, we were able to see the different colours, shapes and sizes of their bodies. When he was ready to head to the field where the apiary is located, I beat a hasty retreat to the house and hid. He returned an hour or so later with three supers. These are the boxes on a bee hive that have frames where the bees store the honey. Each hive was left with one brood box (the larger one on the base) and one super filled with frames that were loaded with honey to ensure that the bees would have enough to see them through the winter and early spring. After all, there is no point in investing time and money in setting up an apiary, if you then take so much honey that the bees can't survive another year!

One super, which was from Andy's hive, was placed into his car. He then methodically and calmly extracted the honey from the frames of our two

supers. He had also removed the honeycomb that the bees had made in one further super, so that I had several kilos of honeycomb filled with sweet flowery honey. Andy worked into the late evening, once the sun went down, he worked by the lights of the barn and the floodlight in the yard.

All had gone smoothly; I hadn't been chased by bees and I was delighted with how much honey there was. Unfortunately, as Andy returned the supers to the hives, he was stung several times on his face and head. He had carefully put the hood back on to protect himself, not realising that a few bees had settled on his hood while he'd been extracting the honey. So, there he was, in the dark of the field, with half a dozen unhappy bees inside his protective bee suit! When he returned to the house, I offered antihistamines, paracetamol and tea. Using tweezers, I removed the stings that were still in his face, neck and head and we talked for a time and drank the tea, to make sure that he was okay and would be safe to drive back home.

My caution and fear of honey bees remains and with each step forward, I take half a step back. In the future when the orchard and food forest are more mature, the honeybees will help pollinate the fruiting trees, but after five years of hosting bees on our homestead, I am still not sure that I want an apiary at Byther Farm. On the other hand, I really appreciate a year's supply of honey!

FORAGED FOOD

Throughout most of the year there are foods that can be foraged from the hedgerows, woodlands and verges all around us.

I find so much pleasure in 'free food', but I am particularly careful to only gather what I'm sure is non-toxic. For this reason, I don't harvest mushrooms at all. There are friends who have identified different types of fungi as we have wandered around our new homestead, but I still leave them in situ and don't take the risk. There are plenty of other sources of free food around us that I am certain are safe to eat. From flower petals to berries, leaves to seeds, there is a wild larder all around us.

Blackberry picking has always been a summer and early autumn activity for our family. My grandson has stoically stood to his hips in long grass at risk of being stung by nettles to reach blackberries to add to our foraging basket. Moments like these are special, spanning the generation gap with shared pleasure and purpose. Invariably, we return home with dark purple stains on our fingers and the purple colour of our tongues is evidence of fruit enjoyed.

Blackberries are not the only fruits that we forage. Elderberries are gathered for making wine, syrups and jellies, and sloes for creating sloe gin. Rosehips, from both domestic and wild plants, are gathered and frozen immediately, only using them once I have enough for a batch of wine or syrup. We also gather hazelnuts and haws, if the squirrels don't take them all first.

I don't forage from nearly as many plants as I could, and if it's something you are really interested in, there are plenty of books to guide you through a foraging adventure.

Do not eat anything picked in the wild (or in your garden) unless you are sure that it is safe to eat. Be wary of taking advice from non-experts or those who offer their opinions via the internet!

What to sow in August

- [ ] Beet – leaves and beetroot
- [ ] Carrot
- [ ] Summer radish
- [ ] Pea
- [ ] Spring cabbage
- [ ] Kale
- [ ] Winter spinach
- [ ] Chard
- [ ] Winter lettuce
- [ ] Chinese cabbage and kale
- [ ] Spring onion
- [ ] Perennial onion
- [ ] Parsley
- [ ] Cilantro | coriander
- [ ] Winter radish
- [ ] Potato in containers
- [ ] Turnip
- [ ] Fennel

ANNUAL CYCLE RACE

With another full circle around the sun completed, I can assess how much food has been or is still waiting to be gathered, processed and stored away to see us through the winter, the hungry gap and into those few sunnier months when the majority of our food takes ten minutes to get from the ground to our plates. My body's posture has gone from hunched against the wind and rain to upright and open, and back again. Plants have appeared from below ground, raced skywards and retreated once more having spread their seeds far and wide. Wildlife has raised another generation of offspring and the rhythm of life continues around us.

Celebrating each part of the annual cycle brings with it a sense of gentle and grounding satisfaction. The very act of being outside, connecting with the world around us and becoming part of our environment, can lift our mood, soothe tensions and feel liberating. And, whether we are actively gardening and growing food or buying it from a local store, the pattern of the changing seasons offers us the opportunity to treat our senses to an ever-changing blend of experiences.

Growing your own food is a personal process and potentially a political one too. The more food that we grow, forage or swap to eat or store, the less dependent we become on commercial forces and the more we can stand outside 'the system'. I have no desire to withdraw from that system entirely; it offers me security for health services, water and energy supplies and a whole host of other benefits that are not immediately obvious. I have no desire to 'stick one to the man', but I do want more control over what I eat, what has been sprayed onto my food and how it is processed. The best way for me to do that is to grow and harvest a wide variety of crops and learn how to store them at home. So, while I am gaining a huge amount of pleasure from tending to the garden, I am also carrying out a very quiet, peaceful and joyful act of rebellion.

Possibly as important as food production, has been learning to celebrate the patterns in the cycle of the year and to enjoy each season for what it is. How I respond, internally and externally, to changes in light levels, rainfall and temperatures is now as important as how much I achieve. While I rejoice in harvesting fresh foods that tingle the taste

buds today or that I will savour in months to come, I also revel in resting and allowing myself to recuperate during the months with far fewer natural daylight hours.

Gardening is not difficult and it is not terribly complicated. It is as problematic as we allow ourselves to perceive it to be. When we stop looking at problems and start seeing possibilities, our whole perspective can change. Our growing spaces stop being places where so much work needs to be done and become places with so much potential to enjoy ourselves.

When I let go of the need to control everything in the garden, when I realised that I'm never going to be a neat and tidy hedges type of gardener, and gave myself permission to enjoy the seemingly chaotic jumble that nature creates, gardening became more and more pleasurable. This does not mean I never try to control some areas of the garden or that I merrily allow weeds to rampage through the vegetable or flower beds, although that happens sometimes. But it does mean that I prioritise watching birds feed from seed heads over cutting the plants back, removing the seed heads and tidying up. It means that I allow the grass to grow longer than a neatly clipped bowling green and enjoy the wildflowers that appear as if by magic. It means that I don't feel obliged to adhere to some 'do this now' formula and instead, I watch and listen to the clues and cues offered by nature.

Nor does growing your own food and flowers need to be expensive. Manufacturers and distributors of gadgets, tools and other garden paraphernalia will entice you to spend your money with them. Some carefully considered items of equipment are undoubtedly worth purchasing, but many can be found secondhand or even being given away. Plants and seeds can be purchased, swapped or propagated. If you are prepared to wait a little longer (and sometimes a lot longer) for the results, your garden, plot or balcony can be filled for very little cost. Neither do you need to wait until you can buy a plot of land. Gardening can be done on any scale, small or large. Whether you are growing in eggshells on a windowsill or an allotment or community garden plot, a balcony of pots and containers or a small bed in your friend's garden, from a sunny backyard to acres of north-facing, windswept hillside, each growing space has potential and excitement.

Creating the new garden in Carmarthenshire has been an interesting and life-affirming experience. It has confirmed to me that I'm one of those people that creates a small growing space and fills it with plants, rather than preparing the whole garden area before I start planting. But luckily, neither of these methods is right or wrong, simply different. And the differences between those approaches might reflect our personalities, our preferred styles or other factors, like time constraints. Whatever the way we garden, thank goodness we do.

As the years pass at what seems an increasingly rapid pace, the feeling of accomplishment at growing our own food rarely dwindles. And I still happily take the credit for nature's capacity for abundance despite my interference!

REFERENCES, GRATITUDE AND RESOURCES

BYTHER FARM

Our website, bytherfarm.com
Follow our continuing journey via the YouTube channel, youtube.com/LizZorab
Or on other social media
Patreon, patreon.com/LizZorab
Facebook, facebook.com/BytherFarm
Instagram, instagram.com/Liz_Zorab_Byther_Farm
Byther Farm is not currently open to the public for visits.

GRATITUDE

Thank you for reading this book. I hope you have found something to make you smile, some new snippets of gardening information and inspiration.

Thanks to Maddy and Tim Harland for your kindness and guidance, and for laughing with me.

Thanks to all the team at Permanent Publications for your patience and enthusiasm.

To Tanya, thank you for your kindness, support and gentle wisdom.

To Huw, my continued gratitude for your friendship, laughter and encouragement.

Cecily, thank you for your love, laughter and being there whenever I need to chat.

My constant gratitude and love to Mr J.

Additionally, Mr J and I thank the community of viewers of our YouTube channel and supporters on Patreon.

And one final thanks to all the women across the world who, in the face of adversity, run small farms and grow food. You continue to be my heroines.

IMAGES

All images in this book were taken by the author except where stated. Cover photo by Jason Ingram. Thanks to Mr J, Niall, Saronne, Geoff, Kathryn, Chillichump and Anna for the use of their beautiful photographs.

YOUTUBE CHANNELS THAT INSPIRE ME

Happen Films
Huw Richards
Lovely Greens
Permaculture Magazine
Self Sufficient Me
The Seasonal Homestead
The Kiwi Grower
You Can't Eat The Grass

INDEX

Enjoyed this book?
You might also like these
from Permanent Publications

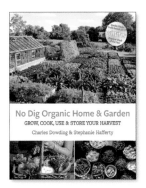